DATE DUE

**GREAT WRITERS** **SYLVIA PLATH**

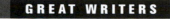
# SYLVIA PLATH

Peter K. Steinberg

Foreword by Linda Wagner-Martin

CHELSEA HOUSE
PUBLISHERS
A Haights Cross Communications ◆ Company

Philadelphia

**CHELSEA HOUSE PUBLISHERS**

VP, NEW PRODUCT DEVELOPMENT Sally Cheney
DIRECTOR OF PRODUCTION Kim Shinners
CREATIVE MANAGER Takeshi Takahashi
MANUFACTURING MANAGER Diann Grasse

**Staff for SYLVIA PLATH**

EXECUTIVE EDITOR: Matt Uhler
ASSOCIATE EDITOR: Susan Naab
EDITORIAL ASSISTANT: Sharon Slaughter
PRODUCTION EDITOR: Megan Emery
SERIES AND COVER DESIGNER: Takeshi Takahashi
LAYOUT: EJB Publishing Services
COVER © Bettmann/CORBIS

A Haights Cross Communications Company

http://www.chelseahouse.com

First Printing

9 8 7 6 5 4 3 2 1

Library of Congress Cataloging-in-Publication Data

Steinberg, Peter K., 1974-
  Sylvia Plath / Peter K. Steinberg.
     p. cm. — (Great writers)
  ISBN 0-7910-7843-4
  1. Plath, Sylvia—Criticism and interpretation. 2. Women and literature—
United States—History—20th century. I. Title. II. Great writers
(Philadelphia, Pa.)
  PS3566.L27Z895 2004
  811'.54—dc22
                                    2004001980

*In loving memory of my grandfather, Elias Steinberg.*

# TABLE OF CONTENTS

A note about the text: Throughout the book I have referenced Sylvia Plath's *Journals*. The edition referred to is the unabridged edition, published as *The Journals of Sylvia Plath* by Faber and Faber in April, 2000, in the United Kingdom. Anchor Books published the same book in the United States in October, 2000, under the title of *The Unabridged Journals of Sylvia Plath*. Pages numbers between the year 2000 editions correspond. The references and page numbers must not be confused with *The Journals of Sylvia Plath* as published in an abridged format by The Dial Press in 1982.

PUBLISHERS HAVE RECOGNIZED that the world of book buyers maintains consistently high interest in the stories of people's lives. Biography or autobiography, memoir or life accounts—these books often sell better than many first or second novels. So because readership exists for life writings, they are published. They are reviewed in the best newspapers and journals, and they are sometimes even sold to film makers.

While it is easy to see the appeal of an exciting adventure narrative about mountain climbing, it is more perplexing to see why a brief life like that of Sylvia Plath not only initially attracts the reader, but continues to attract readers more than 40 years after her death in 1963. Perhaps there is a kind of archetypal story to which we all respond, regardless of generation, profession, or gender. The story of Sylvia Plath, the brilliant woman writer who was a suicide at thirty, poses a conundrum: like moths to a candle, we are wrenched by the evidence of all that promise, in both poetry and fiction, and also in the lives of her two small children—promise wasted in her death. We keep reading the biographies of Sylvia Plath as if we are desperate to find a different narrative, as if pouring *our* energies into her life will create a new ending for it: like the phoenix, perhaps the next biography of this talented American writer will give us more understanding of the poet who dared to proclaim, in the midst of the fogs of suburban convention, dressed in an apron of carefully chosen huswifery, "Out of the ash/ I rise with my red hair/ and I eat men like air."

In Plath's 1962 peom "Lady Lazarus," she stripped postwar American culture of its platitudinous façade: she proved to readers that a woman's life could fill with both rage and blessing. In the poem she tells her readers that an average woman's life could usurp the narrative of a powerful Biblical character: we believe that the resonant woman writer could become her own "Lazarus." By adding "Lady" to the Biblical name, Plath brought the symbol for resurrection into our average women's lives. Her use of the name was a new kind of parody, but rather than aiming for a comic effect, as does much parody, she drew poignance. Even as her readers saw the innate powerlessness of the pretty, well-educated woman character of child-bearing age, they adopted her claim to power: they wanted her to rise, they wanted her to succeed. As Plath did in countless of her late poems, those written between 1961 and early 1963, she here created a fantasy that drew so heavily on the human condition—particularly on the woman's condition—as to be immediately recognizable—and therefore unifying. Compelled to join with this poet, drawn to her voice through the sheerly implausible metaphors she chose to use, readers felt the life narrative of the woman persona as if it were also theirs.

Given today's wide readership for any book having to do with Plath's life, it is well to remember that's Plath's literary career was startlingly brief. Except for single poems and stories, she had published only one collection of poems (*The Colossus* in 1960) and—under the pseudonym of "Victoria Lucas"—her only novel, *The Bell Jar*, barely two weeks before her death on February 11, 1963. Both books were well-received, but in a politely traditional way. None of Plath's readers in the early 1960s was much excited about her work.

By 1965, the year her estranged husband, Ted Hughes, brought out *Ariel*, a partial collection of her late poems, readers began to recognize the mandala-like quality of her art. Plath's idiosyncratic and sometimes parodic voice found an echo in the expression of many of her readers: it was the decade of the 1960s, marked by Betty Friedan's book, *The Feminine Mystique* (1963) and by the tumult of radicalization of society, both through civil rights activity and feminism. *Ariel* eventually attained best-sellerdom. Then in the sixteen year hiatus before Hughes published Sylvia

Plath's *Collected Poems* in 1981, *The Bell Jar* appeared in the United States and most of Europe (under Plath's name), becoming a classic of comic reflection: readers learned that women's lives could be bawdy as well as suffocating. Anything J.D. Salinger had achieved in his *The Catcher in the Rye* a decade earlier was meat for Plath's quirkily self-reflexive fiction.

When in 1982 the Pulitzer Prize for Poetry was awarded to her *Collected Poems*, an award rarely given posthumously, the serious accolades for Plath's craft—and her voice and her strangely prescient consiousness—began. At this time, the nearly unanimous acclaim for her poetry erased some of the stigma of her late poems having been taken as feminist bywords. By the mid-1980s, in fact, Plath and her work had developed a cult-like following, one which made difficult Ted Hughes' life. Hughes, a fine poet who had recently been chosen England's Poet Laureate, seldom gave readings of his own poetry or translations, because many in the audience attacked him with questions about Sylvia Plath; he also endured the defamations of Plath's modest grave marker, when the third name ("Hughes") would be removed, leaving only "Sylvia Plath." Such acrimony complicated literary dealings with Hughes and his older sister Olwyn, who served during these years as executor of Plath's esate; even simple permissions requests might take three or four years to be acknowledged.

By 1989, despite permissions difficulties, three biographies of Sylvia Plath had been published, those by Edward Butscher, Linda Wagner-Martin, and Anne Stevenson. As an index of the high interest in Plath's writing, all three biographies were well-reviewed, and controversies about whose interpretations of Plath's life were more accurate fueled review pages in both the States and England for a number of months.

Still more biographies followed; then in 1993, Janet Malcolm made the study of the existence of so many Plath biographies the topic of her genre-bending *New Yorker* essay, "The Silent Woman." Later in the 1990s, more biographies were published, as were more and more book-length scholarly studies of Plath's work. Interest was heightened even more by the surprise publication, just months before his death from cancer, of Ted Hughes' book

*Birthday Letters* (1998). Hughes' collection of poems written for Plath, or in response to some of her poems, served as a kind of biography as well as a poem collection, charting a narrative of key events in her and his life that sometimes differed from the accounts Plath had herself created earlier in her poems and fiction.

In the twenty-first century, that keen interest continues. Biographer Diane Wood Middlebrook's 2003 study of Hughes and Plath as writers is engagingly titled *Her Husband.*

This biography of Plath by Peter K. Steinberg emphasizes the way her writing was the motivating force of Plath's life. Steinberg gives the reader a compendium of salient facts, all chosen to undergird his careful readings of her work. Though brief, this biography provides a great quantity of useful information and insight, allowing the reader a place of reference before turning back to Plath's work itself.

Linda Wagner-Martin
January 2004

SYLVIA PLATH WAS BOTH an incredibly gifted and controversial poet. Over the last decade, especially since the turn of the century, Plath has been given much needed reconsideration. She had been determined to write and be published in a variety of genres, but especially poetry; by the time of her death, Plath had written poems that would revolutionize modern poetry. In our time her poetry and her novel, *The Bell Jar*, are read and translated around the world. The first translations of her poetry were published in the mid-1960s; her novel *The Bell Jar* was first translated into Polish in 1975. She is undoubtedly one of the most famous and important female poets of the twentieth century, along with Elizabeth Bishop, Marianne Moore, and Louise Glück, to name only a few. Plath became a prominent writer at a young age and continues to be held in high esteem well after her early death by suicide in 1963. (Plath, *Letters Home*, 148)

Most readers first discover Plath in the poetry she wrote near the end of her short life— "Daddy," "Lady Lazarus," "The Moon and the Yew Tree," "Words"—and her life is often seen through her death. Our understanding of Plath comes through hindsight and puts us in a difficult position to determine how much her writing and her death are related. Various library collections and courses taught about her work help us to investigate the complexity of her life and writing. Her friend Jack Sweeney, curator of Harvard's Woodberry Poetry Room, ensured that Harvard University held her first book, *The Colossus*, as early as 1963.[1] This text was also included in a course on modern poetry around that time. The majority of her writing—poetry, fiction, letters, and journals—has slowly been published years, even decades, after her death.

Her work and her death have become so intertwined that they cannot be completely separated. This biography is about Plath's life and writing first and foremost; it will inevitably discuss her death, but not race towards or focus on it. After Plath's death it became fashionable to judge her as a dead poet. For example, a headline in a review of *The Bell Jar* in *Glamour* read: "The Only Novel of the Dead Poet, Sylvia Plath." (Pochoda, 119) However, scholars are now looking closer at her life and the impact of daily events on her work. This discussion will illustrate Plath as a poet, who was concerned with life more than death in her writing. She was a woman and a poet, who could only have written these highly-charged, highly-felt literary works with the knowledge and intimacy of life. Plath has become a multi-faceted figure over time, a controversial, provocative, poet. In many ways, Sylvia Plath has become an icon.

In her lifetime, Sylvia Plath published two books: a book of poems, *The Colossus* (1960/2), and, under the pseudonym of Victoria Lucas, a novel titled, *The Bell Jar* (1963). The book that first brought her to prominence was her second collection of poetry, posthumously assembled and published as *Ariel* in 1965. The poems in the collection include "The Applicant," "Lady Lazarus," "Daddy," "Stings," and "Edge," poems which are striking, lucid, memorable, and unlike any writing before. Their directness on various subjects, their bleak humor and electric, vivid images and sounds drew readers' and critics' attention to *Ariel*. Some critics were taken aback by her work and others were impressed. Fellow poet Anne Sexton, who knew Plath briefly while they were both working on their first books of poetry in Boston in 1959, wrote at the end of her memoir on Plath, "The Barfly Ought to Sing": "What matters is her poems. These last poems stun me. They eat time." (Sexton, 11) *Ariel*, shocking when it was first published, is now a classic; some considered the collection as an early work of feminist literature, and others considered it a milestone in poetry. Today, *Ariel* still leaves its readers stunned and in search of words to describe its effect. Just as important is *The Bell Jar*; when it was revealed that Plath had written the book, the demand for it grew.[2] *The Bell Jar* was eventually published in the United States, becoming a best-seller and another totemic book for the various cults of Plath admirers that arose.

Plath was once viewed as a 'cult' author, but her rise in popularity and fame has drawn more serious attention to her life and work around the world. Though her popularity has led some critics and scholars to dismiss her from the ranks of canonical poets, others are contending that she needs to be studied. Although Plath did not live long enough to amass a wider body of work, she wrote poetry that broke down traditional barriers in striking ways. The direct, vital images and feelings she communicates to the reader are unique and memorable.

## PLATH AS ICON

For many people, Sylvia Plath's iconic status is that of the woman poet, whose life ended tragically when she committed suicide. Arguably, her death has been given more importance than her life. Indeed, her death has been seen, by some, as a way of viewing her entire life. As George Stade writes in his introduction to Nancy Hunter Steiner's memoir of Plath, *A Closer Look at Ariel*: "Our knowledge of her suicide not only clarifies what she said and what she meant—it also certifies that she meant what she said." (Steiner, 3) In other words, many people view her work as being somehow more realistic because of her death. The themes that dominate her poetry are love, death, her children, color, nature, and God. Plath questions, mocks, and deconstructs her subjects. She uses all the colors in the spectrum to further her themes; she most commonly employs the colors white, black, green, blue, red, gray, and yellow. (Matovich, 595–96) However, as Plath's writing continues to be read, interpreted, and understood, her death may eventually be seen for what it was—an event that arose out of complex circumstances that had little to do with her writing. Even her published journals have been labeled as the longest suicide note ever written, though her journals were written over the course of her life.[3]

In the last six months of her life, Plath wrote the majority of the *Ariel* poems, two short pieces "America, America" and "Snow Blitz," commissioned for English magazines, as well as her memoir, "Ocean 1212-W." Plath's writing and her life are very close, but they are not in literal correlation. After *Ariel* was published, Plath was labeled as a 'confessional' poet and her poetry was judged as evidence, as if her life (or rather death) was proof of her character, her life, or the larger world's influence on her. Critics looked at the poetry trying to solve the mystery behind her suicide; this attempt resulted in years of misinterpretation that have left Plath scholars in a morass of assumptions. Words used to define and describe her poetry were 'confessional,' 'dark,' 'feverish,' 'horrifying,' 'murderous,' 'ruthless,' and 'tragic.' (Newman, ed., 289) Therefore, Plath's first acknowledgement as an icon set her as an anguished, hysterical woman, as the woman who wrote *Ariel*, and then suddenly died, leaving these poems in her wake.

In the mid-to-late 1960s, starting with the U.S. publication of *Ariel*, the feminist movement seized upon Sylvia Plath as an inspiration and heroine. She was a significant woman writer, whose life they could point to as a part of the problem, if not the whole problem, of gender inequality. One view of Plath limits her to the roles of a good wife and mother, who suffered after her famous husband, Ted Hughes, committed adultery. Her death was seen as Hughes' fault; the basic male-female relationship was the focal point of the problem because it was not equal enough. However, Plath's life cannot be summed up in this neat, stereotypical way. Her writing should not only be considered feminist, but also feminine. The statements made through her poems and her suicide need to be considered in the context of her entire life.

However, a number of people found it easier to attack Hughes than evaluate Plath's life as a whole. Hughes found himself accused of Plath's death; feminists attended his readings and heckled him. Even today some view Hughes as guilty of mistreating Plath and consider her death an act of vengeance against him and his mistress, Assia Wevill. Biographies of Ted Hughes have been published and present his side of the story to the reading public.[4]

However, after such a long time, the iconic status of Plath will be hard to change. She will continue to be seen as a girl abandoned by her father, a young woman who tried to kill herself, and who later succeeded in her suicide attempt. She was a girl who started publishing poetry when she was eight years old, did well enough in high school to win a scholarship to college and graduate, and made writing her life's vocation, dying shortly after finding her true voice.

Sidestepping Plath's iconic status is difficult, though, since many are reluctant to let go of the romantic view of her death. In this respect, her literary status is close to that of Virginia Woolf (coincidentally the woman writer that most influenced Plath). Just as Plath is known for having died by gas poisoning in her kitchen, Woolf is known for having drowned herself in the local river by her home. In 1956, Plath wrote in her journal of feeling a kind of electric connection to Woolf. Comparing her August 1953 suicide attempt to one of Woolf's, Plath reflected: "Bless her. I feel my life linked to her, somehow. I love her ... but her suicide, I felt I was reduplicating in that black summer of 1953. Only I couldn't drown. I supposed I'll always be over-vulnerable, slightly paranoid. But I'm also damn healthy and resilient." (Plath, *Journals*, 269) As an ultimate tribute, she purchased a stack of Woolf's books from two local Cambridge booksellers, Bowes and Bowes, and Heffers. She read Woolf savagely, striving to perfect her own craft. Scholars are investigating Woolf's influence on Plath's life and work. This aspect, like many others, of Plath's life is challenged by the mythic quality surrounding her death; her life remains mysterious as long as her death takes precedence.

The mystery of her life is alluring to readers and scholars. The desire to know how Plath developed from a good into a great writer draws more attention to her life. How could someone who once wrote to herself, "I am middling good." (*Journals*, 618) suddenly write, "I am a genius of a writer; I have it in me" years later? (*Letters Home*, 468) This cannot be fully explained. To say that she worked very hard is not satisfying enough, though her writing process was significant. Plath wrote and rewrote her stories and poems and was determined to publish them and be read. This ambition kept her going through many difficult times, as her journals and letters indicate. Throughout her literary life, dating back as early as her high school writing, Plath was never satisfied with a completed poem or story. Very frequently, she would discount any older writing in favor of something new. After receiving news that her short story, "Den of Lions" would be printed in *Seventeen*, she said she felt sick as she "reread the paragraphs of lyrical sentimentality that seemed so real and genuine a few months ago." (*Journals*, 38) During an interview in 1962, Plath complained about the entire content of *The Colossus*, her first collection of poetry, when comparing them to her recent poems. She said, "I can't read any of the poems aloud now ... They, in fact, quite privately, bore me." (Orr, 170)

In 1952, just after winning the *Mademoiselle* contest for college fiction, Plath met a working writer, Val Gendron, whose industry and success inspired her to write 1,500 words a day—a tough goal, but one that Plath, strived to maintain. (*Letters Home*, 92) Sylvia Plath relied on mentors for feedback and encouragement, and she was fortunate to always be in supportive company. When she met Ted Hughes, he quickly became her biggest influence and audience, even through the tumultuous portion of their marriage in 1962. One telling anecdote comes from a friend of Hughes', David Ross, who recalls:

> Sylvia was going on about her Olivetti 22 typewriter, and how she'd worn out the roller in a year. Now the roller on my Olivetti 22 never showed the slightest sign of wear, even after many years of use. Sylvia was resolutely determined to make her mark on the literary world, and also that Ted should. (Feinstein, 97)

Plath's and Hughes' relationship, both personal and professional, requires further inquiry to perceive how Plath's writing was impacted. While there is no specific critical journal published about her work, critics and scholars have steadily continued to write articles, essays, and books about her life and work since the late 1960s. Her fame has brought her into popular culture as a poet; she is a symbol of depression and death for some and an angry, brilliant voice for others. She was the only female poet listed in the 'Best Poets of the 20th century' in *Time* magazine, and one of the few poets in the *Ladies' Home Journal*'s "Most Important Women of the 20th Century." She has been mentioned on a variety of television shows including *The Simpsons, Cheers,* and *Dawson's Creek.* Rock bands like the Bangles ("Bell Jar") and the Manic Street Preachers ("The Girl Who Wanted to be God") have written songs about her; another group, the Blue Aeroplanes, set her *Ariel* poem, "The Applicant" to music. Modern composers have done the same, from Elizabeth Swados to Ned Rorem to Shulamit Ran. There is almost no part of culture, "high" or "low," that has not in some way referred or reacted to Plath's story and work. In 2003, the novel *Wintering* by Kate Moses was published. The novel is about Plath's life during the period of the *Ariel* poems' composition, presenting the degree of hope and courage in these poems that had long since been ignored. Countless poems have been written about Plath; her husband, Ted Hughes, wrote an entire book, *Birthday Letters,* to and about her. Other poets who have written about Plath include Richard Wilbur, Anne Sexton, Muriel Rukeyser, Carol Rumens, Diane Wakoski, John Berryman, Stevie Smith, and Anne Stevenson. A number of adaptations for the theater have also been performed on stages worldwide. Some have incorporated her own words, while others have taken more liberty in their reconstruction of Plath's life and feelings. In 2003, Gwyneth Paltrow played the role of Sylvia Plath in the Focus Feature's film, "Sylvia."

Plath has become an icon of American womanhood, a figure out of a Henry James novel: the young American woman who travels to Europe and comes to a bad end. After her death, her writing continues to emerge, slowly, "finger by finger," as she wrote in "A Birthday Present." (*Collected Poems,* 208) In the mid-1990s, a children's story was found in the archive at the Lilly Library, Indiana University. *The It-Doesn't-Matter Suit* was written in 1958 and its discovery lends hope that more material may one day be found. Almost everything that Plath wrote has been published and a far wider collection of her work is held at the following archives: Mortimer Rare Book Room, Neilson Library,

Smith College, Northampton, Massachusetts; the Lilly Library, Indiana University, Bloomington, Indiana; and at the Robert W. Woodruff Library, Emory University, Atlanta Georgia. There are smaller holdings at Washington University, St. Louis, Missouri; The British Library, London, England; University of Texas, Austin, Texas; and Cambridge University, Cambridge, England. (Tabor, 149–152)

By investigating the works of Plath, her biographical material, and new research about her, this analysis will try to answer the question: Who was Sylvia Plath? In a crucial sense, Sylvia Plath's writing was her life. We can trace Plath's life through her published works. She wrote about her life by transforming it into art. The marriage to Ted Hughes helped to bring Plath to her fullest potential. Although they separated in September 1962, Plath forged ahead throughout the autumn of that year to produce a narrative as strong as she was.

# CHAPTER ONE

# Becoming a Poet

*But life is long. And it is the long run that balances
the short flare of interest and passion.*

—Sylvia Plath

SYLVIA PLATH WAS BORN at 2:10 P.M. on October 27, 1932, in
the Jennie M. Robinson Memorial Building of the Massachusetts
Memorial Hospital in Boston's South End. She weighed eight
pounds, three ounces, and was twenty-two inches long. Plath's
parents were Otto Emil Plath (1885–1940) and Aurelia Frances
Schober (1906–1994). Otto was born in Grabow, Germany,
which is located on the Elbe River, roughly midway between
Berlin and Hamburg in an area of Germany called Ludwigslust.[1]
Otto's original surname Platt means 'flat' or 'low.'[2] Aurelia was
born twenty-one years later in Winthrop, Massachusetts, to Frank
and Aurelia Schober. Otto and Aurelia met at Boston University
where Aurelia was registered to take a course he was teaching in
German. At the end of the year Otto asked Aurelia to accompany
him to a weekend in the country at the farmhouse of some mutual
friends; it was at this getaway that Otto and Aurelia fell in love
with one another. (*Letters Home*, 8–10)

Aurelia, an avid reader and an admirer of fine literature, and
Otto, one of the world's leading scholars on bees, always had

plenty to talk about. They were both teachers, she at the high school level and he at the university. Otto Plath had been married before, but was estranged from his wife when he and Aurelia were courting. In order to marry Aurelia, they both traveled to Carson City, Nevada, in January 1932, to obtain a legal divorce. Otto and Aurelia married immediately and soon started a family, for Sylvia was born ten months later.

Aurelia, Otto, and Sylvia lived at 24 Prince Street in Jamaica Plain, a suburb of Boston, which borders a large pond. The Plath's lived on the ground floor of a Philadelphia-style, two-family house with a large front porch on a quiet street within walking distance to both the pond and the Arnold Arboretum.[3] The Arboretum, founded in 1872 and the first of its kind in the United States, was an idyllic place for the Plaths because of its many species of trees and plants and its affiliation with Harvard University.[4] Due to Otto Plath's scientific background, living near the Arboretum and Jamaica Pond made sense. Otto was an expert on bees, and wrote a landmark book on the subject, *Bumblebees and Their Way* in 1935.

Otto and Aurelia loved Sylvia, but Otto also wanted a son; exactly two and a half years after the birth of Sylvia, Warren Joseph Plath was born at the Faulkner Hospital in Jamaica Plain on April 27, 1935. Just over a year after Warren's birth, the family settled in a brown stucco house at 92 Johnson Avenue which is located on the waters edge of Winthrop Bay, Aurelia's hometown. The house had views of both Logan International Airport and downtown Boston, which is a more dramatic view now with the tall office buildings clustered near the harbor. It is also a very short drive to the beaches facing the Atlantic Ocean. Aurelia believed she needed the help of her parents in caring for her children while Otto worked in Boston. From a practical standpoint, living closer to Aurelia's family was a deciding factor in the move, despite the longer, more arduous commute for Otto. Aurelia grew up in Winthrop, and her parents still lived there, at 892 Shirley Street, an oceanfront property, with views of the ocean and bay, on a narrow strip of land called Point Shirley. The two houses were separated by only a few miles, so it was relatively easy for the two households to visit and assist each other. Otto was estranged from his family and made no known attempt to contact them after 1930, but he and his wife were very close to the Schobers. These family ties were important for Plath as a child.

Plath would later claim that her first memory was of the ocean. In the beautiful "Ocean 1212-W," a prose piece commissioned toward the end of her life, Plath slightly modifies her childhood in Winthrop to suit her creative intention while also revealing some deeply buried emotions. In Sylvia's memory, she never lived away from the seaside at any time during her first nine years. Her description of the ocean being "like a deep woman" is telling. She continued, "It hid a good deal; it had many faces, many delicate, terrible veils. It spoke of miracles and distances; if it could court, it could also kill." (Plath, *Johnny Panic*, 21) She respected the ocean like a mother.

The tone Plath uses in "Ocean 1212-W" changes dramatically in her memory: "Then one day the textures of the beach burned themselves on the lens of my eye forever. Hot April." (*Johnny Panic*, 22) With such a foreboding introduction the reader may choose to exercise caution when reading on, not thinking for a moment that such a scorching statement could be about a newborn sibling. Plath continued, "My mother was in hospital. She had been gone three weeks. I sulked. I would do nothing. Her desertion punched a smoldering hole in my sky. How could she, so loving and faithful, so easily leave me?" (*Johnny Panic*, 22–3) Upon receiving the news that a baby was coming into her life Sylvia remembered, "As from a star I saw, coldly and soberly, the *separateness* of everything. I felt the wall of my skin: I am I. That stone is a stone. My beautiful fusion with the things of this world was over." (*Johnny Panic*, 23) Fortunately this grudge, remembered over twenty-five years later, had passed.

Life in Winthrop was not immediately easy and the six years the Plaths spent there were both glorious and tragic. Almost as soon as the family settled in their house, Otto began showing signs of fatigue and stress. In her long introduction to *Letters Home*, Aurelia details her husband's demise: "It was heartbreaking to watch a once-handsome, powerfully built man lose his vigor and deteriorate physically and emotionally." (*Letters Home,* 18) It was the beginning of the demise of Otto's health.

As the daughter of two extremely intelligent parents, Sylvia began reading at a very early age. She won her parents' praise, which encouraged her to learn more and at a faster pace. Aurelia's values in a close, tight-knit family were passed on to Sylvia and Warren. The Plaths were friendly with their neighbors; especially the Freemans, who lived up the block at 8 Somerset Terrace. Sylvia's and Warren's first playmates were Ruth and David Freeman; both sets of children were roughly the same age, although Warren was the youngest.

Sylvia was a very bright student from the beginning, receiving straight A's, which impressed her teachers and family. Sylvia started school in 1937 at the Sunshine School, 77 Bartlett Road. She then attended the Annie F. Warren Grammar School in Winthrop Center from 1938 to 1940, and the E.B. Newton School from 1940 to 1942.[5] From an early age, Sylvia had responded favorably to stories and poems read by her mother. She had been writing poetry from an early age and this resulted in her first published poem, which appeared under the simple title of "Poem" in the *Boston Herald* on August 10, 1941.

Between 1936 and 1939, Otto became more fatigued and more irritable. Sylvia would spend many days and nights nearby at her grandparents' house at Point Shirley. Letters were exchanged between Aurelia and her daughter; they demonstrate the closeness between the two. In mid-February 1940, Sylvia sent one of many letters from her grandparents' house to her father. In this particular letter, she wrote using crayon, and as she mentioned a particular color, she wrote in the corresponding crayon. This is a good example of Plath's creativity and precociousness. Sylvia also decorated the letters she was sending to her father, mother, aunt, and other family members. She cut one letter in the shape of a heart and on another she drew her aunt flying. The bond in the family, especially with her grandfather, grew only tighter through these experiences, as Aurelia wrote, "he not only played games with her but took her swimming with him." (*Letters Home,* 22) Otto's illness prevented him from spending quality time in rearing his daughter.

In August 1940, Otto stubbed a toe on his left foot and shortly thereafter developed gangrene. Incapacitated by pneumonia, he spent two weeks at the hospital in Winthrop. Accompanied by a nurse, Otto entertained his daughter only briefly through the days of September. Sylvia, writing poems and drawings pictures, gave them to her father, which pleased him to no end. (*Letters Home*, 22–23) By October, gangrene had set in so badly his doctors decided he needed to have his entire left leg amputated. Possibly the last time Otto saw his children was in early October, just before he went into the hospital in Boston, for he never returned home. Otto Plath died in the New England Deaconess Hospital on November 5, just nine days after Sylvia's eighth birthday. Throughout his illness Otto had refused to see a doctor, thinking he was dying of cancer, just as a friend of his had. (*Letters Home*, 23) His autocratic, stubborn German mindset contributed to his early death, he was fifty-five years old. Because the family attended the Methodist Church, in Winthrop Center, Otto Plath's funeral took place there. He is buried in Winthrop Town Cemetery on Azalea Path; his headstone, first in its row and along the path, reads, "Otto Plath / 1885–1940." Sylvia never understood why her father died, or at least she did not immediately understand. She insisted that her mother sign a contract vowing never to remarry, which Aurelia did without reservation. (*Letters Home*, 25)

Two years after Otto's death, the Plaths and Schobers sold their two Winthrop houses and moved inland to Wellesley, Massachusetts, a suburb less than fifteen miles west of Boston in 1942. The families moved into a white, clapboard house at 26 Elmwood Road, on the corner of Elmwood and Ingersoll Roads. The house, with its lush green lawn, screened-in porch, and single car garage was the archetype of American suburbia. The move was to benefit the children's health and education. Wellesley had a higher social class and standard of living than Winthrop, and Aurelia was hopeful Sylvia might win a town scholarship to Wellesley College. Aurelia knew one family in Wellesley, the Nortons. William Norton and his wife Mildred had three young boys, Richard, Perry, and David, and lived a couple of miles away at 47 Cypress Street. William Norton had been a colleague of Otto's at Boston

University and the families would become so close that the children considered themselves cousins and addressed the parents as 'Aunt' and 'Uncle'. At this time Aurelia, whose religious beliefs were rooted in the Unitarian Church, began attending the local Unitarian Church on Washington Street, just outside of the town square. Winthrop had lacked a Unitarian Church so she and the children attended religious services at the Methodist Church. An added bonus was that the Nortons were also Unitarian. Unitarianism, which practices the belief in one God and not three representations, would later be Sylvia's favored religion.

Sylvia, who had started schooling at an early age, was held back one grade upon arrival in Wellesley in order to keep her in class with children the same age; she was ten at the time. The school system in Wellesley was also completely different than that of Winthrop's, so the decision to hold Sylvia back would also enable her to adjust to the system. At the Marshall Perrin Elementary School, Sylvia repeated the fifth grade, excelling as usual despite the new course material. She was an enthusiastic student, completing forty book reports in the school year; she also enjoyed the Girl Scouts. (*Letters Home*, 30)

Beginning in the summer of 1943, and continuing for the next six summers, Plath attended three different summer camps. She first attended Camp Weetamoe at Center Ossipee, New Hampshire, just roughly fifty miles south of Mount Washington in 1943 and 1944. Plath sent dozens of pre-stamped postcards home, meticulously telling her mother what she had been eating and her activities. Her attention to detail was extraordinary. The campers enjoyed arts and crafts, water sports, and competitions throughout the summer. The camp itself was on the edge of a lake with inspiring mountain views.

By the time Sylvia entered the Alice L. Phillips Junior High School in 1944, she was certain she would achieve success in artistic fields, notably art and writing. Aurelia encouraged Sylvia to write by placing diaries in her Christmas stocking each year. In these diaries, Sylvia would record her daily activities at school and time spent with friends, quite typical for a twelve-year-old girl. They are an important starting point for her creativity, teaching her by virtue of practice to notice details and accurately log them with pen and paper. She also decorated journal pages with her increasingly competent drawings. At this point, she was more mature as an artist than a creative writer.

Continuing her fine scholastic record, Sylvia found the time to write poems for submission to the school newspaper called the *Phillipian*. Between 1945 and 1947, Plath had a total of fifteen poems and at least one story and one article published as well. An example, from the November 1945 issue of the *Phillipian* is Plath's poem, "My Garden,"

> In the corner of my garden
> There is a favorite spot
> Which sun and rain tend faithfully
> And which I planted not.
>
> Here is the haven of wild flowers,
> The kingdom of birds and bees,
> Where in the sil'vry moonlight
> Sprites dance 'neath singing trees. (*Phillipian*, Nov. 1945, 7)

Sylvia would try writing poems, stories, and articles for the *Phillipian* and her English classes. Other poems she was writing and would publish are titled, "The Spring Parade," "March," "A Winter Sunset," "The Snowflake Star," "Fireside Reveries," and "Sea Symphony," to name a few. The titles suggest that they are poems written by a teenager, but Sylvia's proficiency, even in these early poems, is quite remarkable. Plath received many honors and certificates for her scholastic achievements. At the end of seventh grade, Plath received an "Honor Certificate for Reading," which was given to a student for reading ten books of which at least two were non-fiction. She also received three "Commendation" cards for her creative writing talents, for her contribution to class discussions, and for her handling of War Stamp sales.

A year later Plath would write what may be considered her best early poem, "I Thought That I Could Not Be Hurt." In this poem she exhibits an extraordinary sensitivity to an inadvertent action by her grandmother. The speaker of the poem is lifted up by a wonderful day in which she feels nothing can go wrong. Plath writes, "Then suddenly my world turned gray, /and darkness wiped aside my joy." (*Letters Home*, 34) She calls her grandmother's action "careless" but accepts her remorsefulness as genuine. Plath's achievements were acknowledged again throughout her eighth and ninth grades; she was given another four Honor Certificates for reading, as well as commendation cards for spelling, for receiving straight A's and B's, and for winning an unprecedented six school letters.

During the next two summers, 1945 and 1946, Plath attended Camp Helen Storrow at Buzzard's Bay, Massachusetts. She continued her detailed letter writing home, now using pen instead of pencil and her handwriting much improved. Plath averaged one letter a day to her mother. The postcards had faded out of use, replaced by letters, whose limitless space for writing proved advantageous for Plath's daily correspondence. At camp they made crafts, swam according to ability, rowed boats, and hiked for miles at a time around Long Pond and Fisherman's Cove. Plath particularly enjoyed the arts and crafts sessions and was encouraged by her counselors to take art lessons. Plath's love of the ocean was rekindled, partly because the camp was near the ocean, and because her childhood friend from Winthrop, Ruth Freeman, was at the camp too. Aurelia also spent time away from Wellesley, enjoying time away in Chatham, Cape Cod and at Star Island, off New Hampshire.

Plath's sense of humor and interest in different people is noted throughout her early journals. On August 13, 1947, upon seeing a set of twins who came to paint the Plaths' house with their father, she remarked how bizarre twins seemed. To her amazement, she could be on either side of the house and see identical people. Eight days later she had gotten a bad haircut and her best friend's mother fixed it. The trauma apparent in the journal is appropriate for a fourteen-year-old who was just weeks away from entering high school.[6] Plath's best friend throughout her Wellesley years was Betsy Powley, who lived nearby at 57 Parker Road.

When Sylvia entered Wellesley's Gamaliel Bradford High School, now called Wellesley High School, she was even more determined to hone her skills as a writer and an artist. Sylvia's English teacher was Wilbury Crockett. Crockett was a demanding teacher who asked little more from his students than to care and to try. He would be Sylvia's English teacher the entire time she was a student at the high school. From early on in their relationship, Crockett recognized Sylvia's poetic gift, especially in "I Thought That I Could Not Be Hurt." He would encourage her to send her poems to magazines and newspapers for publication. Sylvia collected dozens of rejection slips, but the rejections did not discourage her at all; instead, they made her try even harder. Little did she know that the determination and consistency she was practicing would be a lifelong habit. If one magazine did not like what she wrote, she would immediately send it out again to a different one.

The realized threat of the Cold War and the atomic age, which was going on in the heart of Plath's adolescence and young adulthood, prompted her to interview a leading expert on the atom bomb. Plath published a front-page story called "The Atomic Threat" on her mother's birthday, April 26, 1948. As far as scholars can tell, this was her first printed political opinion. Previously, in 1944, Plath wrote a poem called "A Wish Upon a Star." This poem, written toward the end of World War II, illustrates a pacifism she would hold throughout her life. Plath's political mentality and involvement has been largely ignored; but, as she matured, she grew into a very concerned mother and citizen.[7]

In June 1948, the school announced that Sylvia was one of several students in the Advanced English program at Bradford High School to be recognized in a national contest sponsored by the *Atlantic Monthly*. Sylvia submitted two poems, "April, 1948" and "The Farewell," and received two merit awards. At an early age Sylvia was determined to be accepted professionally by national magazines such as *The Atlantic Monthly* and *The New Yorker*; although she knew that starting at the top was unrealistic, she tried anyway.

Sylvia Plath spent the summers of 1947 and 1948 at the Vineyard Sailing Camp at Oak Bluffs, Martha's Vineyard, off the coast of Massachusetts. Plath took a train from Boston and then a boat across the Cape Cod sound. Plath began decorating her letters and envelopes with drawings; she asked her mother to save postcards and letters so she could add them to her diary later. Betsy and Ruth both joined Plath during the summer of 1948 at the camp. In addition to sailing, Plath biked around Martha's Vineyard, and continued to write poems and stories, and gain experiences that she could use in future work.

Plath's writing was developing rapidly; indeed, she seemed to have written all through high school. The archive at the Lilly Library has many stories and poems written by Plath while she was in high school. They show, more than anything else, her early dedication to the art of capturing life in her writing. She was even exploring the subject of her father; in a story called "Sarah," Plath's protagonist's father accidentally hacks his leg off with an ax.[8] Each story uses techniques she learned from reading stories printed in popular women's magazines such as *Seventeen* and *Mademoiselle*. Gradually, as Plath developed as a writer, her stories moved from being almost pure description, to including dialogue and tension. The only stories from this time ever printed are "The Green Rock" and "A Day in June," both written in 1949. In "The Green Rock," Susan and David return to their childhood home near the sea to visit their aunt after five years away. On the way there, Susan daydreams about what it was like when they played along the beach and pretended that a large green rock jutting out of the sand was their castle, mountain, or sailboat. On actually being there, seeing their old home repainted, and the beach and rock much smaller, they become disappointed. Plath frequently visited Winthrop, primarily in the summertime, to see old friends. No doubt as she grew older, some memories of her childhood days lost significance.

Plath spent part of the summer before her senior year at Bradford High at a Unitarian retreat on Star Island. (Aurelia stayed at Star Island during the summer of 1946.) Star Island is one of the nine rocky islands that collectively make up the Isles of Shoals eight miles off the coast of New Hampshire. This retreat marked, perhaps, Plath's last participation in organized religion. Plath drove from Wellesley with Rev. Bill Rice, the minister of the Wellesley

Unitarian Society, and sailed on a boat called the "Kiboko" on June 26, 1949. She lodged with a roommate at the old Oceanic Hotel on Star Island; the girls outnumbered the boys and other than reading prayers, the main activity was dating. Although there is not an existing manuscript of the story, Plath did make notes towards a story, which would feature a boy-crazy teenage girl spending a week on the island.

Back in Wellesley for the summer, Plath played tennis, dated several boys and often returned home after midnight. She spent time dancing at the King Phillip Club, on the shore of Lake Pearl in Wrentham, Massachusetts, or at the Totem Pole, another night-club, or she went driving around through the suburbs. She tried alcohol over this summer, and in her journal, discusses her own budding sexuality. The dates she went on that summer sparked curiosity, not necessarily about having sex, but about the limits imposed on herself as a young adult. She railed against the double standard, which allowed boys to experiment sexually and look down upon participating girls.

As a senior at Bradford High, Plath maintained her academic excellence. Throughout most of the autumn, Plath did not keep a journal, presumably to spend her time studying and dating. As her high school career came to a close, she was not without reward. She was a National Honor Society member and received a history prize from the Sons of the American Revolution, as well as honors from a regional art contest and recognition from the *Boston Globe* for journalism and poetry.

In 1950, Plath, now a senior, progressed as a professional writer, publishing her most provocative work to date. Her hard work and dedication was rewarded by having short stories and poems accepted and published in the *Christian Science Monitor* and *Seventeen*. Plath was very active on *The Bradford* school newspaper. Not only did she write a number of articles and serve as co-editor, she also contributed a number of poems. She co-authored with Perry Norton an article printed in the *Christian Science Monitor* called "Youth's Appeal for World Peace," which urges pacifism. The two young authors try to persuade the President to consider changing his stance on using atomic energy. They argue that, "it seems inconsistent to undertake the construction of a weapon designed to kill more people more efficiently," and that democracy and capitalism can spread more effectively through consultation and peace. (*Christian Science Monitor*, March 16, 1950, 19) Many of the poems Plath published in the school newspaper that year reflected her growing command of subject and content. Poems such as "Complaint," "The Farewell," and "Family Reunion" are balanced with joy and pain, a poetic formula Plath would learn to explore more deeply as an adult.

Plath's high school report card was nothing short of impressive. In academic courses she received straight A's. In secondary subjects, such as orchestra and physical education, her performance was still impressive with a steady B grade. On three different Intelligent Quotient, or I.Q., tests Plath scored 140, 134, and 143. All three scores placed her above the 98 percentile; her intelligence level was that of a genius. She graduated as the number one student in her class and as the recipient of many school achievement awards. Sylvia Plath would leave a mark on Bradford High School, even having an annual poetry award given in her honor.

Sylvia's hard work in high school was rewarded in her choice of colleges. One of the motivating factors in Aurelia Plath's decision to move to Wellesley had been the presence of Wellesley College. Wellesley College accepted students on full scholarship from Wellesley, and Mrs. Plath hoped that Sylvia, who was showing academic progress from an early age, would qualify. In November 1949, Bradford High sent Smith College, in Northampton, Massachusetts, a transcript of Sylvia's grades. They would send two additional transcripts in the winter and spring of 1950. The only other transcript was sent to Wellesley College in March 1950. Smith College, a girls-only school like Wellesley College, was Plath's first choice. In her home at 26 Elmwood Road, Sylvia had to share a room with her mother, which she must have found embarrassing as a young adult. Being accepted to Smith College, with financial aid in the form of scholarships, would allow her the opportunity to live away from her family for the first time, aside from the summer camps.

Plath's 'mature' journals start in July 1950 during this transition from high school to college.[9] Her first entries are mostly undated and full of reverie and drama; they are short recollections of passing moments occasionally lengthy when an important experience occurred. Sylvia Plath aimed to capture her life in words, no matter how mundane her thoughts or opinions, in the attempt to get to know herself, her history. The act of writing was almost as important as what she was writing. Plath's journals eventually became workbooks, full of longer entries of self-castigation and creative ideas. They contain poem and story concepts that were familiar to her readers long before the *Journals* were made public.

During the summer of 1950, Plath worked at Lookout Farm in Natick, Massachusetts. She and Warren lived close enough to the farm that they could bike from their house. However, Plath writes in her journal that they would bike to Wellesley College, roughly half way, and then get a ride to the farm from there. During the summer, Plath met an Estonian artist called Ilo Pill, who lived in the farm's barn. One afternoon in August, Ilo lured Plath to his room and kissed her, much to her surprise. In her journals, Plath wrote a long, emotional entry about the incident even though she was afraid she to "over dramatize it or underplay it" and "exaggerate the wrong parts or ignore the important ones." (*Journals*, 10) The incident scared her, but it also gave her an electric shiver. (*Journals*, 11)

From the standpoint of creativity, the summer of 1950 was successful. The experience of picking fruits and vegetables on the farm made its way into a poem and a non-fiction article. The *Christian Science Monitor* printed the poem, "Bitter Strawberries" and the article, "Rewards of a New England Summer" in August and September. *Seventeen* accepted Plath's short story, "And Summer Will Not Come Again" for their August issue, after holding it for over a year. The story was written about her experience with John Hodges, a former boyfriend, during the summer of 1949; this was her first professional acceptance. Later, in November, her poem, "Ode to a Bitten Plum" also appeared in *Seventeen*, marking her first professional publication as a student at Smith.

Plath received a fan letter from Eddie Cohen of Chicago in early August 1950. He confessed to reading the story in his sister's copy of *Seventeen* and found it more remarkable than other stories he had read. They began an intense correspondence; a blizzard of letters was sent between Chicago and Boston. He wanted a friend to write to and asked that she send him more poems and stories. There were very few topics they left untouched; Cohen was several years older than Plath and sexually experienced, which provided her the opportunity to discuss the topic openly and at a safe distance. One of their more passionate discussions was about war. They were both pacifists and, in a letter to Cohen, she expresses deep fear and concern about herself, her family, and opportunities that may be "cut off" from their lives. (*Journals,* 19) She felt these fears deeply. She was also only a month away from entering her freshman year at college.

Smith College, one of the most prestigious women's colleges in the United States, accepted Plath in May 1950. She received $850 financial aid in scholarship money in the name of Olive Higgins Prouty, a very successful novelist and Smith graduate. At the time Plath was awarded the money, the two women had little knowledge of each other, but this would soon change.

# CHAPTER TWO

# Climbing the Ranks: Plath at Smith

*So I am going to one of the most outstanding colleges
in America; I am living with two thousand of the
most outstanding girls in the United States ... The
main way I can add to my self-respect is by saying
that I'm on scholarship, and if I hadn't exercised my
free will and studies through high school I never
would be here.*

—Sylvia Plath, *Journals*

IN HER JOURNALS, PLATH EXPRESSED anxiety a few days before
leaving for college. In a long, undated September entry she tells
herself to remember a date she had been on before the collegiate
onset of "confusion, dilemmas." The date would be her last with
that particular young man; that she decided to break off the relationship days before does not come as a surprise. And it is not the
only time she would abruptly end a relationship with a man.
Plath's journals often probe her rationality regarding men and
dating. They are also frequently very self-critical. It would be fair
to say the seedlings of Plath's later poems like "Mushrooms" and
"The Applicant" were planted as early as 1950.[1] She constantly
looks toward beginnings; for Plath, everything mattered.
Inevitable crises appeared and disappeared; people came in and

out of her life. Plath was pragmatic enough to write down everything as carefully as she could and was both sensitive and resilient enough to move on when necessary.

Shortly before entering Smith, Plath wrote a story called "Den of Lions." The story closely echoes Plath's break-up with a young man she was dating. In the story, Emile and Marcia are on a date with some friends at a club.[2] Emile is attractive and Marcia is interested in him. Marcia realizes that Emile moves in different social circles than she does, and their love ends shortly after it begins. In the *Unabridged Journals of Sylvia Plath*, the eleventh entry details a double date at a club called Ten Acres with a young man called Emile. That evening Plath addressed herself as "the American virgin" before leaving for an evening filled with sexual tension. (*Journals,* 13) The practice of writing stories and poems that mask real events and people is one that Plath seemed interested in perfecting and would do so with time. She seemed to be leading a double life by molding stories to suit her needs.

A careful reading of Plath's journals and letters at this time will give the reader much information about her first Smith days. In late September, in keeping with her summer camp tradition, she was writing a letter to her mother every day. Initially Plath was concerned about getting along with her housemates in Haven House, decorating her room, and learning the ways of a Smith girl. She got along wonderfully well with her roommate, Ann Davidow from Chicago and several other first-year students.

Haven is a large, yellow house with a front porch at 96 Elm Street, Northampton. Plath resided at Haven for her first two years at Smith, retaining a room with a view of Paradise Pond. The campus at Smith College was built on a hill. College Hall was built dramatically on the incline with a large gate at the entrance off Elm Street. The Neilson Library and a number of academic buildings were built behind College Hall, comparatively at the crest and flat of the hill. Student houses were built along Elm and Green Streets, which split near College Hall forming two boundary roads for the campus.

Plath had conversations with herself in her journals about her classes and social situations. She deliberated the existence of God, life after death, and even her own ability to achieve a God-like status. (*Letters Home*, 39–40) At times there may not be anything extraordinary about her journal writing, but at all times life is being processed on the page. Throughout the fall, the torrent of letters she and Eddie Cohen were writing continued. Early in their correspondence, they began discussing taboo topics such as sex. While Plath abstained from sexual intercourse for fear of pregnancy or being stigmatized, Eddie had a little experience. Their discussion influenced Plath's confusion over how far to go and not wanting to be labeled. While Eddie was falling madly in love with Plath, she fell in love with only the idea of him. She held herself back from deeper emotions, enjoying their kinship through the letters, but he wanted to meet her. Keeping Cohen at a distance through letters enabled Plath to focus on her other duties at Smith.

As the recipient of the Olive Higgins Prouty Fund scholarship Plath was encouraged by the admissions office at Smith to write a thank you letter to Mrs. Higgins Prouty for the endowment. Mrs. Higgins Prouty, born in 1882, lived at 393 Walnut Street, Brookline, Massachusetts, just miles from Plath's home in Wellesley. She wrote *Stella Dallas* (1923), which was turned into a radio series broadcast for eighteen years. She also wrote *Now, Voyager*, which was a successful movie starring Bette Davis. Her novels were based on some of her own experiences as a woman, and one who had had a breakdown.

Plath met Mrs. Prouty in December at her Brookline home. The meeting was a very important one for both women. Prouty was the embodiment of a successful writer. She was sophisticated, generous, kind, and wise. Plath wrote "Tea with Olive Higgins Prouty" shortly after the meeting.[3] In the article, Prouty advised Plath to use her own life as material for stories. Although Plath was already writing in this style, getting confirmation, or permission, to write in this manner boosted her self-confidence. In the article, Plath admitted that she had difficulty sounding credible when writing about travel and adventure because she had little to no experience.

Plath left the meeting and immediately took the advice to heart. Stories such as "Den of Lions," "Initiation," and "The Perfect Setup" were published in *Seventeen* over the next two years. Poems too, like "Twelfth Night," "White Phlox," and "The Suitcases are Packed Again," also received national attention in the *Christian Science Monitor* and *Seventeen*. She had found a formula and style that enabled her to take various experiences and write about them seriously and successfully.

The spring semester of Plath's first year at Smith passed by with dates and classes. She also had a new roommate named Marcia Brown.[4] In early January 1951, Plath received news that her story, "Den of Lions" had won third prize in *Seventeen*'s fiction contest, bringing in $100. Plath was a rising star on campus with the success she was having on a national level; her growing fame brought the kind of attention college administrators would enjoy having on campus. She started writing drafts for poems in her journals, too. Although Plath studied and wrote a lot of the time, she had caught the eye of Richard "Dick" Norton, her longtime acquaintance from Wellesley, and a senior at Yale University. Their relationship soon developed.

In early February, Plath went with Marcia to her aunt's house for a skiing weekend in Francestown, New Hampshire. One of the biggest events of the semester took place when Plath went to Yale, in New Haven, Connecticut, to spend the weekend of February 17, with Dick Norton. Plath stayed at a house called "the Coop," at 238 Prospect Street, near Yale's chemistry building. Together with Dick's younger brother Perry, they watched a swim meet on campus and got to know each other better. Norton also invited Plath to the Yale Junior Prom, held in early March.

Norton was studying to be a doctor and represented the ideal man of the 1950s. He was an intelligent, handsome young man with a great future ahead of him, and Plath was surprised that he was interested in her. Plath and Norton spent time with each other at dances and plays in either Northampton or New Haven. Plath's journals record the romance with great detail and act, for the first time, as a workbook for later writing material.

After the weekend at Yale for the Junior Prom with Norton, Plath captured the thrill of it in her journal; the weekend was romantic and dreamlike. On Saturday night, she and Norton walked back to her lodgings from the town after seeing a play. They detoured, at Norton's suggestion, to see the view of the city from a steep hill behind Yale's chemistry laboratory building. Plath was beside herself with joy when she wrote about the event in her journals; ten years later she satirized the event, remembering it at a cool distance in *The Bell Jar.*[5]

Later in March, at the beginning of her spring break, she planned to visit Marcia in New Jersey and tour New York City for the first time. What she did not plan on was Eddie Cohen driving from Chicago to meet her and take her to Wellesley. The meeting was largely disappointing as Cohen was exhausted and Plath was shocked at his sudden arrival. Her aloofness toward Cohen may have been a result of her dating Dick Norton. However her relationships with the two men developed, Cohen and Plath's letter-writing resumed.

Though her love life seemed to be falling into place, Plath was still undecided as to what her major would be in the spring semester of her first year. She equally enjoyed creative writing and art classes and debated the pros and cons of majoring in each. In mid-May, however, she informed her mother that she would major in English. Along with this decision she concentrated on finishing the year and finding a job for the summer.

Plath and Marcia were hired as babysitters in Swampscott, Massachusetts, an ocean-side suburb north of Boston. Plath lived with the Mayo family at 144 Beach Bluff Avenue; she began work on June 18, 1951. Marcia lived with a family a few houses away at 100 Beach Bluff. Both houses were a short distance to Phillips Beach; Plath even had a view of the ocean from her second-floor bedroom. Her room featured a door off a balcony that looked over a long, sweeping grass yard, leading to the ocean. The experiences she had over the summer caring for three children and doing household chores did not come without stress. Shortly into her job she wrote a letter to her mother asking for advice and help with various daily issues, such as how to handle the troublesome children and learning how to cook.

Plath and Brown had ample time to bond over the summer. On July 24, a day off, they rented a boat in Marblehead Harbor and rowed out to Children's Island, a rocky, wave-beaten island off Marblehead Neck. They were reading Philip Wylie's 1942, *Generation of Vipers*, a book which is critical of the American way of life. Ten years after that summer experience Plath wrote "The Babysitters," a serious poem recalling a time of lost innocence. "The Babysitters" is a slightly exaggerated poem about that summer; but it also contains a good deal of information. Plath credited Marcia with getting the better house to baby-sit in, lamenting the lost time. By the end of the poem, especially, the reader begs for more detail; according to Plath, "Everything has happened." (*Collected Poems*, 175)

As Plath's sophomore year approached, her journals suddenly turned further inward. In a single entry in September, 1951, she explicates her feelings on her selfishness, vanity, and jealousy of men. Under the social pressures of the 1950s, Plath felt trapped by the unwritten requirement that a woman be educated and then immediately packaged into a marriage and life as homemaker. Plath's summer experience as a babysitter prepared her for some of these future duties. The questions she asked herself always led to writing, and whether or not she would always be free to pursue it.

Back at Smith, Plath spent several days in the school infirmary in October. She met with a representative from *Mademoiselle*, who was touring colleges to meet prospective students for their College Board Contest. Her fall academic schedule—including courses in government, art, creative writing, English literature, and religion—was very demanding. Spending time recuperating invariably meant missing out on time for coursework.

The *Christian Science Monitor* ran Plath's "As a Baby-Sitter Sees It," a two-part article about her summer experience, in November 1951. Although Plath changed the names of the family and children, she otherwise related a story that seems true enough based on her journals and letters. The two-part article also printed three of Plath's original sketches, one of each child she minded. The sketches show a competency parallel to the writing in the article. What is clear is that Plath, honest reporter to herself, had begun to write about her life more and more freely. This article by Plath represented the third article published by the *Christian Science Monitor* in eighteen months.

Plath wrote another story about babysitting called "The Perfect Set-Up" in October. This story is more challenging, confronting issues about family values and intolerance. Based on Plath's experiences, the story's morally difficult situation faced by the protagonist made it a success. Plath wrote stories with this kind of formula and found that magazines were more interested in them. The story was awarded honorable mention in a *Seventeen* short story contest and published in October 1952. Plath was also working on her poetry at this time. Her poems of choice were sonnets, but she was also trying other poetic forms such as the villanelle and sestina. Although she did not publish much, she was writing poems and often including them in letters to her mother and in her journal.

Plath's relationships were also sources of her writing. While Plath was in Marblehead, Norton worked as a busboy on Cape Cod. The distance between the two damaged their relationship. Norton would later confess to having a love affair with another woman during the summer of 1951, which would damage it even further. As Plath was debating the difficulty she had dating in her journals during the fall of 1951, she declared how hard choosing a mate was. Plath even asked herself, "Why can't I try on different lives, like dresses, to see which fits best and is most becoming?" (*Journals,* 101) Throughout her sophomore year, Plath continued dating Dick Norton, who by this time had entered his first year at Harvard Medical School in Boston.

In the spring of 1952, Plath was in the second semester of her sophomore year. She was recognized several times with honors at Smith College. She was elected as Secretary of the Smith College Honor Board, which oversaw honor code infringements and decided on penalties. She was elected to the Press Board. Plath's role in the press board got her regional exposure in newspapers such as the *Daily Hampshire Gazette,* the *Springfield Daily News,* and the *Springfield Union.* Plath was a member of the Press Board until 1954. To reward Plath for her excellence in creative writing, she was also elected to Alpha Phi Kappa Psi. She was later elected to the editorial board of the *Smith Review*, a journal that showcases Smith students' creative works. The semester went by so quickly that Plath only wrote two entries in her journal before July.

By early April, Plath had written a story called "Sunday at the Mintons'" and planned to send it to *Mademoiselle*. The story was Plath's best to date and, in a letter to her mother, she reveals that her intention was to make it psychological, incorporating wish-fulfillment. (*Letters Home*, 84) In the story, Elizabeth Minton has returned home to live with her older brother, Henry. Henry is very stiff and mathematical, almost mechanical in his actions and thoughts. He is very concerned with directions and punctuality, while Elizabeth is not. On a routine walk along the ocean Elizabeth dropped her mother's broach onto the rocky shoreline. The tide was coming in fast and strong; Elizabeth was worried the waves would sweep it away. She imagined that Henry had gone onto the rocks to save the pin and was swept away by a great wave. As the story ends though, Elizabeth is roused from her vision by Henry. The story is loosely based on her relationship with Norton and exhibited the weakness of her feelings; the relationship stalled as it reached its high point in the first year.

Due to the distance between Plath and Norton the previous summer, she sought to be employed on Cape Cod. Plath applied for and was accepted to work at The Belmont, a hotel in West Harwich, Massachusetts. She started working in early June and was placed at the hotel's side hall because she had no previous experience as a waitress. She would not only serve employees, but also clean dishes and move tables; she was disappointed because she would be earning far less money from tips. During June, Eddie Cohen traveled back to Massachusetts again to meet Plath. He had been writing letters that expressed his interest in meeting her again, for another chance.[6] Eddie was torn between the two versions of Plath, the young woman in the letters and her physical presence. He became more enamored than ever before, but was mature enough to offer her advice on her own dating problems.

Shortly after Plath arrived at the Belmont, Aurelia forwarded a telegram from *Mademoiselle* announcing that her story, "Sunday at the Mintons'," had won a $500 prize for their College Fiction contest. The telegram requested she mail a photograph and biographical note immediately since the story would be published in their August issue. *Mademoiselle's* August issue, with its focus on the collegiate scene, was edited each June by college students from across the country. Winning the prize ensured that Plath would have enough money for her first semester as a junior. Had any qualms about being a writer or an artist still existed in Plath's mind, this singular achievement encouraged her to become a professional writer.

The stress of working long hours, seven days a week, took its toll on Plath by early July and she came down with a sinus infection. She decided to leave the Belmont and return to Wellesley to recover. As she regained her health, she began to regret telling the hotel she would not return. Plath read an ad for a "college-age girl" to be a mother's helper in the *Christian Science Monitor*. The girl, according to the ad, had to be "neat, intelligent, and of pleasant disposition." (*College-Age Girl*) By July 11, Plath had arranged to interview with the Cantors in Chatham, Massachusetts, ten miles from the Belmont.

Working with the Cantors at their summer home on Bay Lane, Chatham, was infinitely more important to Plath than her previous job at the Belmont. Like her previous experience with the Mayo family, Plath was welcomed into the Cantors' family life. The beach was a short walk away, as was the Chatham Bars Inn, a local hotel. Plath also spent time driving and walking around Chatham, going to Oyster Pond and Hardings Beach. She took care of three children again, though the oldest child, Joan, was only seven years younger than Plath. The Cantors practiced Christian Science and although Plath read the *Christian Science Monitor*, entries in her journals confess that she knew little about the religion. As the summer progressed in Chatham, her award-winning short story, "Sunday at the Mintons'" hit the newsstands. The *Christian Science Monitor* printed her poem, "White Phlox" on August 27, her first poem published in nearly a year.

Back in Wellesley for a few weeks before the semester started, Plath prepared for a science exemption examination. If she passed the exam, she would be able to take a different course, most likely in English or Art. The demands she made on herself were too rigid, and she decided to rest before returning to Smith. Later in September, Plath met with Wilbury Crockett for a few hours. He planted the seed in Plath's mind about applying for a graduate study fellowship at either Cambridge or Oxford. Plath had at least two years to work toward England, but immediately she was concerned about money. She had made $1000 for her writing since her senior year of high school, but her mind was set racing at the thought of England; her journal entries became more concerned about money and men. Perhaps most importantly, the prospect of England brought closure to her failing relationship with Dick Norton.

At Smith, for her junior year, Plath moved to Lawrence House, a four-floor, red brick cooperative residence on Green Street. Lawrence House was closer to the shops and the library, and, although Plath lost her view of Paradise Pond, the move signified her own advance in the Smith ranks. Plath had to perform duties around the house such as waiting on tables and being on house watch. With "Sunday at the Mintons'" in print, the reputation Plath was making for herself as a writer continued to grow. The *Smith Review* reprinted "Sunday at the Mintons'" and *Seventeen* also published Plath's short story, "The Perfect Set-Up" and the poem, "Twelfth Night."

Despite the period of rest she had just prior to the school year, the demands of her junior year started to accumulate. Plath dropped her Art II class in favor of devoting time to her elected duties on the Press Board. She also received word that *Seventeen* accepted her story called "Initiation" and that it had won third prize in a contest. "Initiation" was first conceived as a potential story when Plath met with Olive Higgins Prouty in December 1950. The story is about Millicent, a high school student much like Plath, who had to endure five days of social torture and embarrassment as part of her initiation into a popular, powerful group of high school girls. She comes to the moral realization after being accepted that the sorority was intolerable to her and she quits. By the end of the story, with egg drying in her hair, she emerges from a darkened basement as her true self.

In early November 1952, Plath made one of her first references to committing suicide. Norton had contracted tuberculosis during the fall and was sent to rehabilitate at a hospital in Ray Brook near Saranac Lake, in upstate New York. A combination of Plath's challenging academic schedule, worrying about Norton's health, and her extracurricular activities left her too exhausted to sleep.[7] Plath was very hard on herself around this time, calling herself a "conglomerate garbage heap of loose ends." (*Journals,* 150) She also began to question her identity, asking and wondering repeatedly who she was. It was also during this period, with Norton away, that his letters to her became decidedly more emotional.[8] While at Ray Brook, he had little to do and wrote to Plath almost as habitually as she wrote to her mother.

Plath spent the Thanksgiving holiday at home in Wellesley. She met Myron "Mike" Lotz, a roommate of Norton's, and began dating him within a few months. Over the winter holiday, Plath and Norton traveled to Ray Brook, where he tested negative for full-scale tuberculosis. It was the first time she had seen him in over two months, and according to her journals, she did not feel the same emotions toward him as she had earlier in their relationship. (*Journals,* 155) During the visit, Plath went skiing and after colliding on the slopes, suffered a broken leg. In *The Bell Jar,* this scene is recreated and it symbolically breaks all her ties with 'Buddy Willard'; this was likely the case in real life, too. While both she and Norton would recuperate in time, their relationship would not.

When the second semester started at Smith, Plath was in a cast. She found getting around campus difficult. She convinced herself that she broke her leg as a symbolic act for breaking up the relationship with Norton. She was increasingly agitated and exhausted as well, as is evident in many of the journal entries of January 1953. Despite her growing anxiety, she was hopeful to start a relationship with Lotz. Dating him was important to Plath; he proved that there existed someone more interesting and impressive than Dick Norton. Lotz, who pitched for the Detroit Tigers' minor league farm team during the previous summer, proved to be inspiration enough to Plath as he gave her someone to look forward to seeing and knowing.

In February, Plath met and also began dating Gordon Lameyer, a senior at Amherst College and a native of Wellesley. Plath wrote her villanelle, "Mad Girl's Love Song" with Lotz in mind, most likely around February 20 or 21, 1953. As far as Plath's poetic development is concerned, this poem is as important as her short story, "Sunday at the Mintons'." Writing "Sunday at the Mintons'" helped Plath reconcile to her lost feelings for Norton; writing "Mad Girl's Love Song" brought a new subject into Plath's poetry: madness.[9] This subject would be integral to Plath's work.

Plath had her cast removed after living with it for nearly two months on February 19, and she was disgusted at her leg's color and shape. She would need to rehabilitate it enough to attend the Yale Junior Prom with Lotz in early March at Yale. Over the several weekends Plath spent with Lotz in either Northampton or New Haven that winter, the dates they went on grew increasingly physical. As intense as these evenings were, Plath had enough willpower to not sleep with Lotz. Throughout the spring, however, Plath dated Lotz and Lameyer, eventually losing interest in both.

Throughout the spring, Plath published poems and articles. In all, Plath published one story, five poems, and at least four articles in local newspapers before the semester was over and continued to gain recognition for her writing. Plath had three poems published in the spring issue of the *Smith Review*: "Mad Girl's Love Song," "To Eva Descending the Stair," and "Doomsday." Plath was on assignment for the Press Board, attending local events and writing articles for the *Daily Hampshire Gazette* and the *Springfield Union*. *Seventeen* printed a sonnet titled "The Suitcases are Packed Again" in their March issue. The sonnet was written in the fall of 1952 as she remembered how frequently she had moved around the previous summer. The poem conveys that no matter what the world brings, be ready to pack up your belongings. *Seventeen* had been publishing Plath's work for nearly three years. In each issue that her work appeared, there was a small photograph and blurb about the author. In April, *Seventeen* published "Carnival Nocturne," which would be the last poem they published by Plath until 1974, when they reprinted "Ode to a Bitten Plum" from their 1950 issue.

Plath enjoyed the arrival of warm spring weather and the blooming flowers. She was planning on spending the first weekend of May in New York City with an acquaintance made the previous summer while on Cape Cod. She wrote her longest short story titled, "I Lied for Love" and hoped to win a contest that the popular magazine, *True Story* was hosting. Around April 24, good news arrived. *Harper's*, one of the big name magazines Plath was sending her poems to, accepted three poems, "Go Get the Goodly Squab," "To Eva Descending the Stair," and "Doomsday" for a total of $100. Plath was still working toward being accepted by *The New Yorker* and *The Atlantic Monthly*. Around this time she wrote a letter to Warren, who had just been accepted to Harvard, pleading with him to help her relieve some stress their mother was experiencing. In the letters Plath was sending home there was a genuine concern expressed for her mother's well-being. While the letters were upbeat, and convincing, Plath's journals expose a growing edginess. In some cases, the journal entries and letters home contradict one another.

More good news was soon to arrive regarding Plath's writing, but she struggled with her emotions regarding two men. Plath was also elected as editor for the *Smith Review* for her senior year and as Smith College correspondent to the *Daily Hampshire Gazette*. Springtime seemed to bring many awards and prizes for her. Throughout all of these busy times, Plath was also writing new poems such as "Admonition," "Parallax," and "Verbal Calisthenics," all poems inspired by Emily Dickinson. The relationship with Lotz was finished by the end of April. Plath reproached Lotz for being unfaithful, but also criticized herself for befriending Lameyer. Lameyer, only weeks from graduating, planned to enter the armed services which involved his being at training camps and leaving for months at a time for tours of duty. Plath's relationships became complicated and unfulfilling.

Plath had more than relationships to occupy her time. Over the summer, she intended to attend Harvard Summer School in July. But, in early May, Plath received word from *Mademoiselle* that she had won a coveted Guest Editor position for the month of June, which meant living in New York for almost the entire month. In her journals, she asked herself, "Is anyone anywhere happy?" (*Journals,* 184) Despite her mounting exhaustion, which was leading her dangerously closer to her breaking point; she began to work on her first assignment even as she was writing her exams. However much she needed to rest, the opportunity to work for a magazine that had been good to her was one she had to take.

# CHAPTER THREE

# The World Split Open

*... I can't think logically about who I am or where I am going. I have been very ecstatic, horribly depressed, shocked, elated, enlightened and ener-vated—all of which goes to make up living very hard and newly.*

—Sylvia Plath, *Letters Home*

WHEN SYLVIA PLATH WON a coveted position as a Guest Editor for *Mademoiselle*, it was the crown of her success after publishing her poems and short stories in young women's magazines. Out of hundreds of hopeful applicants, twenty were chosen from across the country to go to New York City to put together the special August 1953 college issue. Plath found out she had won in May; she had been steadily sending in applications and assignments since the previous autumn. She had only two weeks to get ready; using some of the *Harper's* money she had earned, she bought new clothes for her stay in New York City. Plath was happy to be going, but she also felt as if her life only had meaning if she was writing: "I want to write because I have the urge to excell [*sic*] in one medium of translation and expression of life. I can't be satis-fied with the colossal job of living." (*Journals*, 184)

*Mademoiselle* required Plath to start two assignments before June 1st, when she was expected at their offices at 575 Madison Avenue. She interviewed the Irish novelist, Elizabeth Bowen on May 26, at the Cambridge home of the poet and novelist, May Sarton. A photographer was on hand to take pictures of the two, who seemed to have a good rapport. Her other assignment was to write on five American poets including Richard Wilbur, Alastair Reed, George Steiner, William Burford, and Anthony Hecht, which was called "Poets on Campus" by the magazine. A large packet of materials given to Plath included suggestions for her wardrobe, daily schedule of assignments and events, and a history of the magazine.[1] She was also given a list of local restaurants and their suggestions on how much to tip at restaurants and for taxi rides. She had requested permission to leave New York City the weekend of June 14 to attend her brother's graduation from high school, and Marybeth Little gave her permission, as long as she left the office after four o'clock.

Plath had been to New York City several times since her first visit in March 1951, but never long enough to be touched by the city's magic. The Guest Editors were staying at the women-only Barbizon Hotel, two blocks by six blocks away from the *Mademoiselle* offices. Plath was given room 1511, a small single, with a bathroom and showers a few doors down the hall.[2] Her room overlooked Third Avenue, and she could see the United Nations building and a small portion of the East River. The room was a standard, with a telephone and desk; the carpet was green, the walls beige and the bedspread and curtain patterns matched.[3] Plath got to know the city in a different way, just as she got to know the magazine business and the world of 'femininity' first-hand—a femininity best described as 'pink think': "Pink think assumes there is a standard of behavior to which all women ... must aspire. When you hear the words 'charm' or 'personality' in the context of successful womanhood, you can almost always be sure you're in the presence of pink think." (Peril, 7–8) To be a good writer was required at *Mademoiselle*, as well as proper dress and comportment at all times. As a rule, the Guest Editors were required to wear hats to all public engagements and appearances.[4]

Plath's time at *Mademoiselle* was hectic, in both her own work as Guest Managing Editor (she had wanted to be Fiction Editor) and the many events the magazine arranged, from parties and visits to other magazines and fashion boutiques. Each morning the Guest Editors reported to the office to learn what their assignments were for the day. They were also required to return to the office after each public affair. At a luncheon event sponsored by the advertising agency Batton, Barton, Durstine, and Osborne on June 16, several of the editors, including Plath, came down with ptomaine poisoning, an event that she included in *The Bell Jar*. On Saturday, June 19, they went to a New York Yankees baseball game; many nights were spent at the ballet, movies, and clubs. Plath worked harder than most of her coworkers; she read and criticized manuscripts and wrote blurbs and captions, and rewrote her "Poets on Campus" feature to better suit the *Mademoiselle* style. She did manage to have a couple of evenings with male acquaintances in Greenwich Village, but for the most part Plath's long days of work and social events left her exhausted and disillusioned.

One event that seriously affected Plath while in New York City was the execution of Julius and Ethel Rosenberg on June 19, 1953. The Rosenbergs were sent to the electric chair, having been found guilty of high treason; the couple was convicted for passing atomic secrets to the Russian government so that they could also build an atomic bomb. Their executions caused Plath great anguish, as it did others who felt the two were innocent or to those opposed to the death penalty. "There is no yelling, no horror, no great rebellion. That is the appalling thing," Plath wrote in her journal. "Two real people being executed." (*Journals*, 541–2) Plath was a pacifist and against capital punishment; the complacency she saw around her was shocking to her. On the morning of the executions Plath could not eat; she was too disgusted. This distress, added to her negative opinion of big city life and work stress, culminated in late June, with a *Mademoiselle*-sponsored dance at the Tennis Club in Forest Hills, Queens, where she was sexually harassed by a United Nations delegate.

Plath's last few days at *Mademoiselle* were just as hectic as her first. She toured the *Herald Tribune* offices, got a behind-the-scenes look at Macy's, saw the play, *Misalliance* at the Barrymore Theatre, and attended a party at one of the editor's houses. Before leaving New York, she ate lunch with Cyrilly Abels, her boss at *Mademoiselle*. Despite being a hardworking and successful Guest Managing Editor and having her poem, "Mad Girl's Love Song," printed in the August issue, the experience was not what she had expected; Plath returned home feeling "young and inexperienced ... in the ways of the world." (*Letters Home,* 120) When she met her mother at the Route 128 train station, she found out that she had not been accepted in Frank O'Connor's short story course at Harvard Summer School, which she had counted on taking. This was as great a disappointment to Plath as the experience in New York City had been. She needed constant reassurance that she was a good, promising, and publishable writer; she thought her failure to win a place in O'Connor's course meant that she had no talent and could not write.

Though Aurelia encouraged her to relax and enjoy herself, Plath could not, and soon began to feel as though she had let down all her supporters and sponsors. She had no desire to read, had trouble sleeping, and had no goals. Aurelia tried to make her feel better by teaching her shorthand, but Plath's writing was not easily adapted to it and she soon gave up, the failure making her feel worse. Plath saw Lameyer in early July; they traveled "to the mountains and the ocean; we talked about Dylan Thomas's poetry and *Finnegan's Wake*; we listened to Beethoven and Brahms symphonies ..." (Butscher, ed., 34) But Lameyer was blind to Plath's increasing depression.

In mid-July, she had purposely cut her leg with a razor, a clear cry for help. Aurelia took her to see the family doctor, who in turn recommended Aurelia take her daughter to see Dr. Peter Thornton, a psychiatrist. Later that month, Lameyer visited the Plath family for the weekend, but still did not notice anything different about his girlfriend, though she was clearly depressed and sleepless by this time. Plath did not discuss her state with anyone but her immediate family and doctors. Dr. Thornton advised that Plath be given electroshock therapy (ECT) and then be sent home, without hospitalization. On July 29, she was given ECT for the first time without any preparations before, such as muscle relaxant or anesthetic, nor did she receive professional care or support afterwards. After several sessions, Plath was worse than ever; the sleeping pills her doctor had prescribed in July were no longer working, and the treatments, actually near-electrocutions, were only making her more withdrawn and depressed. Her loneliness increased, which led to her determination to take her life.

On the morning of Monday, August 24, after having pondered ways to commit suicide (and having failed an attempt to drown that weekend), Plath broke the lock on the box where her mother stored the sleeping pills. She took them and a blanket down to the basement, got a glass of water and put them all in a crawl space usually blocked by firewood. She entered the small space, which was directly underneath the front porch, and blocked the entry with the firewood. She wrapped the blanket around herself; she swallowed forty-two sleeping pills and then lost consciousness. She had left a small note on the dining room table: "Have gone for a long walk. Will be home tomorrow." (*Letters Home*, 125)

Mrs. Plath was frantic; she had found the note after returning home and immediately phoned the police. News of Plath's disappearance quickly spread, with local boy scout troops and the police searching for her all over Wellesley and Boston. Mrs. Plath's panic only increased when she found that the sleeping pills were missing. The *Boston Globe* ran daily articles about the search for Sylvia Plath. "Beautiful Smith Girl Missing at Wellesley" ran their Tuesday headline; another the next day, Wednesday, read "Daylong Search Fails to Locate Plath Girl."[5] Mrs. Plath was quoted in the *Boston Globe* about the possible reasons for her daughter's distress: "She has been unable to write either fiction, or her more recent love poetry ... she believed something had happened to her mind, that it was unable to produce creatively any more." (*Boston Globe*, 1) On the third afternoon, Warren heard a moan coming from the basement. He rushed to the noise and called to his mother to telephone an ambulance. (*Letters Home*, 125) His sister was very ill, but alive. Upon regaining full consciousness, Plath told Aurelia, "It was *my* last act of love." Plath also said "Oh, if I only could be a freshman again. I so wanted to be a *Smith* woman." (*Letters Home,* 125–6)

Olive Higgins Prouty, Plath's sponsor at Smith, once had a nervous breakdown and recovery when she was young and she helped the Plath family immediately with financial and emotional support. Plath had been taken to her local hospital, Newton-Wellesley, for immediate treatment after she was found; she was then given a private room there under a twenty-four-hour watch. Mrs. Plath and Warren both took turns in looking after her. In early September she was transferred to the psychiatric ward at Massachusetts General Hospital in Boston, but she did not improve there amongst the more depressed patients.

During her time in the crawl space, Plath had vomited many of the pills she swallowed. Her body had also convulsed and, in doing so, she had cut and bruised her right cheek just below her eye. The swelling covered her right eye; when she first regained consciousness she could not see out of the affected eye. By the time that Mrs. Plath, Prouty and the head of the psychiatric department decided Plath would recover better in a private mental hospital, Plath's open sore had healed enough for her to see, leaving a large brown scar on her cheek. Plath was admitted to McLean Hospital in nearby Belmont, Massachusetts, in mid-September. Prouty acted as sponsor for her treatment; she was sympathetic to Plath's case. There, as Plath later wrote, "I had my own attractive private room and my own private attractive psychiatrist." (*Letters Home,* 131) The psychiatrist, Dr. Ruth Beuscher (nee Barnhouse) described Plath as being, upon admission, " ... furious. She was angry with her mother. She had too much plain living and high thinking—her words. She had been raised with this intense focus on the thinking function ... which was not her nature ... she was an intuitive, feeling type; she just had an extremely high IQ, that's all." (Alexander, 130)

Plath had lost many vital skills, such as the ability to read, as a result of her suicide attempt. She had many visitors to help her, including Mr. Crockett, her favorite English teacher, who came and retaught her these skills. Mrs. Prouty came to see her progress; she did not feel as if Plath had enough scheduled activities. Gradually,

Plath regained her capacity to read, write and type while at McLean; but she was not improving mentally and was still despondent in early December. As a result, Dr. Beuscher had prepared Plath for shock treatments during her recovery at McLean; these commenced in the middle of the month. Within only a few treatments, Beuscher recalled, Plath "recovered so fast it was obvious that the shock treatment had a psychological significance ... it was almost though she had to be punished for something." (Alexander, 134) The authorities at McLean determined that Plath improved so significantly that she would be discharged in January, 1954, and admitted for the spring semester at Smith. This angered Prouty, especially as Plath was to have no special care upon leaving. Prouty was so upset with McLean that she had stopped paying for Plath to be treated there, but the doctors at McLean found Plath so interesting a case that they took her on for free in January. Plath rested at McLean for most of January until the semester began, since her doctors would not consent to her living at home. She prepared herself mentally to return to the rigors of the academic world.

When Plath returned to Smith in late January, she was welcomed back warmly. She had only three courses that term—European Intellectual History, Modern American Literature 1830–1900, and Russian Literature, focusing on Tolstoy and Dostoevsky. She returned to Lawrence House where she was given her own room, a rarity at the College. Her only duty was to bring the housemother her breakfast tray each morning. She saw the college psychiatrist, Dr. Booth each week and talked with her mother on the telephone often, more for Aurelia's relief. Since Plath had no scholarship, Aurelia paid for her term so that she would not have to worry about money.

Plath had some adjusting to do; she would not be graduating with her class and she had new housemates and fellow students to meet. She also had to get used to going out on dates again. She was still interested in Lameyer, but she concealed the fact that she was dating other boys from him. Her first act of sexual intimacy was with Philip McCurdy during a visit away from McLean on a weekend pass. McCurdy was her brother's age and they had been friends since high school. Dr. Beuscher had encouraged her to explore and express her sexuality as a way to relieve the mental pressures and tensions in her life. She told her mother she intended to date in a more casual, indulgent way, but first she had to reestablish her life at Smith. (*Letters Home*, 143)

By late March, she was back in her routine—she flew, for the first time, to New York City, visiting the Museum of Modern Art for an article she was writing, an assignment for *Vogue's* Prix de Paris competition. She also saw the silent movie, *The Temptation of Saint Joan* and wrote her mother: "After it was all over, I couldn't look at anyone. I was crying because it was like a purge, the building of unbelievable tension, then the release of the soul of Joan at the stake." (*Letters Home*, 135)

With this release, Plath returned to Smith and in mid-April wrote "Doom of Exiles," the first poem she had written in nearly a year. Nancy Hunter, a transfer student who was given Plath's room during the fall semester, gives a portrait of Plath writing:

> She wrote slowly, plodding through the dictionary and thesaurus searching for the exact word to create the poetic impression she intended. Sometimes she chose words with disquieting connotations for their shock value ... [They] could be released only painfully, bit by agonizing bit, as though wrenched free of some massive blockage. (*Steiner*, 43–4)

At about the same time she met Richard Sassoon, a Yale student distantly related to British poet Siegfried Sassoon. Richard Sassoon, "a slender Parisian fellow who is a British subject and a delight to talk to" (*Letters Home*, 136) became her newest boyfriend; his European, literary background (he wrote her letters in English and French) was the exact opposite from any of her previous boyfriends. She continued to write to Lameyer, however, and planned to see him that summer, when his tour of duty was over.

In late April, Plath was awarded a $1250 scholarship from Smith for her next year; the *Smith Review* published several of her poems, and *Harper's* finally ran "Doomsday." Plath had to decide on her senior thesis and chose the theme of the double in two works by Dostoevsky: *The Double* and *The Brothers Karamazov*. Plath considered classmate Nancy Hunter to be her own double and they decided to be roommates for their senior year. Hunter later wrote, "She referred to me in letters to her mother as her alter ego and often remarked that we presented a mirror image or represented opposite sides of the same coin." (Steiner, 41–2) Plath convinced Hunter to take courses at Harvard Summer School in the summer of 1954 and to share an apartment along with two other Smith students in Cambridge. In the meantime, Plath readied herself for summer by sunbathing and reading on the roof of Lawrence House, and as part of her new "casual" look, bleached her hair blonde. While she was attracted to Sassoon and attached to Lameyer, neither of them was available; Sassoon was in Europe and Lameyer's ship was still out to sea.

At Harvard, Plath had two courses; German and the Nineteenth Century Novel, which gave her much to read, including Austen, Stendhal, Balzac, Tolstoy and Dickens. Plath also did the shopping and cooking for her housemates with Hunter, and explored Boston with her in her spare time. They watched sailboat races on the Charles River, bought clothes at Filenes' basement, and stopped at any interesting antique or bookshop that they could find. Neither Plath nor Hunter worked too hard on their courses. As part of their "shop girl mentality," as Hunter put it, was a bargain: "we would accept any and all dates that included an invitation to dinner or the theater, even if we found the men themselves uninteresting." (Steiner, 57) The two "felt safely immune and unassailable" because both were practically engaged to boys back home, and, at first, the bargain worked well and nothing unusual happened. However, in late July, this changed.

Plath and Hunter met a visiting biology professor, whom Plath called Irwin in *The Bell Jar*, on the steps of the Widener Library at Harvard. He went to a diner with them and talked, clearly impressing them with his intelligence; soon he asked both Hunter and Plath out for dinner. On Hunter's date he took her home and, after dinner, chased her, insisting that they have sex. Hunter escaped, and Irwin took Plath out next; at first their relationship was merely friendly, but eventually turned darker. Irwin called to say Plath was hemorrhaging; according to Hunter, Plath returned home that afternoon looking "dreadful ... a chalky pallor lay over her normally tanned skin." (Steiner, 63) Plath had lost a great deal of blood, and when Hunter finally asked her what happened, she replied, "He raped me." Hunter wanted to take Plath directly to hospital, but Plath was horrified at the idea of returning to one; Hunter relented and got instructions from a doctor to help cease the flow of blood. Eventually, however, Hunter calmed Plath down and found a doctor who would help her, and called Irwin to drive them to the hospital; Hunter told the doctor to bill Irwin for the operation. Remarkably, Plath continued to see Irwin after this episode.

It should be noted that while Plath was at Harvard, she saw Dr. Beuscher on a regular basis, and that for a time Irwin drove her to her appointments. Hunter's memoir, *A Closer Look at Ariel*, makes it clear that Plath was rigidly disciplined, but also wanted to explore and have experiences that were out of the ordinary. Plath may have seen Irwin as a combination of these needs, just as he was later depicted in *The Bell Jar*. It is probable she told Dr. Beuscher of the Irwin episode, as she trusted her completely: "I do love her; she is such a delightful woman, and I feel that I am learning so much from her." (*Letters Home,* 140)

Plath returned to Smith in October, concentrating on two objectives: her Fulbright application and her senior thesis on the double. Her other courses for the fall term were Shakespeare and German. She had dyed her hair back to brown, as "with my applying for scholarships, I would much rather look demure and discreet." (*Letters Home,* 144) She had enjoyed being a blonde, but realized that her natural color suited her best. Plath worked hard on her thesis and various applications, trying to get into the graduate program at Radcliffe, the women's college of Harvard, as a safety school. Her courses left her with no time to see Lameyer that fall, except when she went home at Thanksgiving.

That fall, Plath saw two poems, "Go Get the Goodly Squab" and "To Eva Descending the Stair" published in *Harper's,* and her story "In the Mountains," a fictionalized account about visiting Dick Norton at Saranac, published in the *Smith Review.* She also interviewed Alfred Kazin as an assignment for the *Smith Alumnae*

*Quarterly.* Kazin was teaching creative writing and modern literature at Smith and invited Plath to join his course, which she did soon after. In December, Plath was offered a special course in poetics with Alfred Young Fisher, for which she had to write poetry. She was thrilled to be writing creatively in prose and poetry for these professors, as she admired them both for their high standards and intelligence. These professors also admired her and wrote letters of recommendation for her.

But Plath's main goal was still ahead—to attend a university in England, Fulbright scholarship or not: "If only I get accepted at Cambridge ... I really think that if I keep working, I shall be a good minor writer some day." (*Letters Home,* 148) She had set her sights on Cambridge University, but her main worry in being accepted there, or any other program, was not her grades or extracurricular activities, but the stigma of being at McLean and missing her fall 1953 term at Smith.

Plath went to New York City in December to see Sassoon; their affair was now official, and it was an added inspiration for her writing. That she found Sassoon inspiring may have been one of the reasons why she gravitated towards him and away from Lameyer, whom she was fond of writing to but did not provoke any outpourings of poetry.

In January, Plath's schedule for her last term at Smith was set— Fisher, Kazin, Shakespeare, and German. She handed in her sixty-page thesis for review, feeling it was superior work and also qualified as a finalist in *Vogue's* Prix de Paris contest. (*Letters Home,* 150) She was once again sending stories and poems out to magazines and was up early in the morning noisily typing these and new works for Fisher and Kazin. She spent the second to last weekend in New York City with Sassoon, and it was during this visit that she saw the play, *The Dybbuk* by S. Ansky.[6]

In February she heard her first good news—Cambridge University had accepted her as a foreign affiliate for a two-year program; before this news, Plath entertained the idea of teaching in Morocco with her friend, Sue Weller, as she wrote "I am not a missionary in the narrow sense, but I do believe I can counteract McCarthy and much adverse opinion about the U.S." and that she wanted to give back to the world and serve others. (*Letters Home,* 163) In March she heard that Oxford had accepted her as a foreign student as well; it was obvious that her successful recovery at McLean and her return to Smith outweighed her breakdown and suicide attempt. Still, she had no news about her Fulbright scholarship.

Besides the work she was doing at Smith, Plath had little time to socialize. She did manage to see Sassoon in February when her suitcase was stolen from his car. In March she was asked to write a report for *Mademoiselle* on a symposium on "The Mid-Century Novel" at Smith, a day-long event with Kazin, Brendan Gill, and Saul Bellow, and chaired by Mary Ellen Chase. She also continued to work on the Prix de Paris. This constant activity led to another case of sinusitis so intense she had to stay at Smith's infirmary. During one of her periodic visits to the infirmary, she met Peter Davison, then an editor for Harcourt & Brace, and a past recipient of a Fulbright to Cambridge. He visited her on Kazin's suggestion as he was in Northampton touring the area bookstores. He was older than Plath, was literary and traveled; his father, a poet, taught at Hunter College, and he was well-connected. Plath went to one local bookstore with him, deciding she liked him well enough to consider him as a literary contact and a possible romantic interest.

In April, Plath competed in the Glascock Poetry Contest, which pitted her against other college poets in New England. At the host college, Mt. Holyoke, she read her poems for a jury, including Marianne Moore and John Ciardi, and an audience of two hundred. At the end of the competition, Plath and the other poets all recorded poems at a local radio station, making the event the first time she had read her work for an audience and radio broadcast. For Plath, though, what mattered was hearing the other poets, and meeting Moore and Ciardi. Over the course of the weekend she got along well with her roommate, Lynne Lawner of Wellesley College. Even though they never met in person again, they remained close throughout the rest of Plath's life, writing deep and personal letters to each other. Plath was judged a co-winner, something she did not expect, as she felt one of the men was bound to win.

Back at Smith, Plath continued to work on her first poetry manuscript, *Circus in Three Rings*, for Fisher. She dropped her German course in order to have more time to devote to her creative work and studies, as she did not need the credit to graduate; she may have also wanted to improve her average. She submitted "Circus in Three Rings" to *The Atlantic Monthly*, which was willing to print it if she would be willing to rewrite part of the poem and rename it "The Lion Tamer." She was used to either being accepted or rejected, so this odd request flummoxed Plath, who wanted the $25 check but did not want to compromise her writing to go along with publication in this prestigious magazine. (*Letters Home*, 170) Plath responded with a new poem called "The Lion Tamer," enclosed with the original "Circus in Three Rings" and five other poems. A month later, *The Atlantic*'s poetry editor Edward Weeks decided to accept her original version of "Circus in Three Rings." Getting published in *The Atlantic Monthly*, based in Boston, was another milestone for Plath. Although Weeks and his staff confused Plath, the ordeal surrounding "Circus in Three Rings" was a learning experience. She had long tried writing specifically for a market or a magazine and it would be a long time before any other poetry editors would have difficulty with Plath's writing.

While she was busy that spring, Plath had been putting off seeing Lameyer for some time; she and Sassoon had fallen in love, and while she was still fond of Lameyer, she knew their relationship had to end. At the same time, Lameyer, unable to go skiing with Plath, went with another girl and ended up breaking a bone in his hand in an accident; this 'break' was as symbolic for him as Plath's was from Norton two years earlier. (Butscher, ed., 40)

Plath moved forward in her work as well as in her relationships. In May, Plath won an honorable mention in *Vogue*'s Prix de Paris contest; she also won several prizes at Smith, including one based on an anonymous poetry manuscript, as well as two other poetry prizes. *Mademoiselle* accepted "Two Lovers and a Beachcomber by the Real Sea," a poem showing heavy influence from Wallace Stevens. The *Smith Review* published a poem, "*Danse Macabre*" and her short story, "Superman and Paula Brown's New Snowsuit", a deceptively simple story about childhood and the greater political world.

On May 20, Plath received the most important news—she had won a Fulbright scholarship to attend Cambridge University in England. She phoned her mother, who was being treated in the hospital for a chronic stomach ulcer, with the news. Of all the achievements she had worked for, this was the greatest; congratulations poured in from past and present teachers and mentors.

Plath graduated from Smith College on June 6, 1955. One of the honorary degree recipients was Plath's acquaintance from the Glascock poetry competition, Marianne Moore. The commencement speaker was Adlai Stevenson, who encouraged the well educated, even brilliant, class of six hundred to marry and use their hard-won education to create and run households where they could influence the thinking of their families, particularly their husbands. This, Stevenson said, was their "highest vocation" in life. Plath was in definite agreement; she was to interpret his message as meaning that a creative marriage was the highest achievement a woman could have.

Plath spent the rest of the summer writing and socializing. She remained friendly with Lameyer, and in July started to date Peter Davison, who was now an associate poetry editor at *The Atlantic Monthly*; she also managed to see Sassoon, who had been writing her almost daily from New Haven. Plath dated Davison intensely for a month; she was both emotionally and physically intimate with him, but dropped him bluntly one evening. Later she would write of him in her journal: "I was too serious for Peter, but that was mainly because he did not participate in the seriousness deeply enough to find out the gaiety beyond. Richard [Sassoon] knows that joy, that tragic joy." (*Journals*, 206) A few days after she ended things with Davison, she went to Washington D.C. to visit Sue Weller and saw the sights, including the National Gallery, Library of Congress, and the Washington Monument. She returned to Wellesley with Lameyer, who was in the area and was kind enough to drive her back. Back in Wellesley, she formally ended her relationship with him, though they remained friendly for another year through letter writing. After a round of last visits with Prouty, friends, and family, her brother drove her down to New York City. On September 14, from Pier 91, Warren saw her off as the *Queen Elizabeth* set sail with all the other Fulbright scholars.

Aurelia had given Plath dance lessons as a going-away present and, while crossing the Atlantic, she was likely able to put the lessons to good use. On September 20, the ocean liner docked in Cherbourg, France, for one day and Plath became enamored of the small coastal town instantly: "Such warmth and love of life ... Everything is very small and beautiful and individual. What a joy to be away from eight-lane highways and mass markets ..." (*Letters Home,* 182) That evening, the ship sailed to Portsmouth, England, and Plath arrived by train in London, and began her life as a Fulbright scholar.

# CHAPTER FOUR

# Plath in England

*Then the worst happened, that big, dark, hunky*
*boy, the only one there huge enough for me, who*
*had been hunching around over women . . . came*
*over and was looking hard into my eyes and it was*
*Ted Hughes.*

—Sylvia Plath, *Journals*

THE IDEA OF A FULBRIGHT scholarship, of England, and of Cambridge was now reality. Plath believed that now her destiny would be met and played out. (*Journals*, 147–8) She arrived in England, stayed in London for a few days in late September and got to know the city—theaters, movies, pubs, and the Underground. She attended a special party for the Fulbright scholars where they could meet the important literary figures from Cambridge and elsewhere. Plath met a future lecturer, David Daiches, but complained to her mother about the poor service at the event. (*Letters Home*, 182) Only later did she find out that Stephen Spender and John Lehmann were there, and that T.S. Eliot had been invited, but was unable to attend at the last minute. This casual way of dealing with the reception upset Plath, and it was perhaps her first taste of English life and attitudes. For someone who liked to keep busy and have a structured life, the freedom of Cambridge, in comparison to Smith, must have been both liberating and frustrating.

Plath had to adjust to the academic system in England. For her two years there as a student she was enrolled at Newnham College, one of two women's colleges established in the Victorian period; it had only been accepted as equal to the male colleges in 1947. At Cambridge, she had to choose her lecturers; these would lead to the subjects of her exams. "Reading" is the term used in England for majoring in a subject. Plath was reading in English and had two regular courses, Tragedy and Practical Criticism. For these she had to write papers and attend small classes every week; otherwise she was free to attend lectures and read the immense amount of books required for the final exams at the end of her two years there. She had already begun to buy the books by her lecturers, including the influential F.R. Leavis. In her Tragedy course she would read the history of tragedy, from Aeschylus, Sophocles, and Euripides to Shakespeare, Webster, and Racine, and on to more modern dramatists, such as August Strindberg and Luigi Pirandello. The course the English Moralists was unknown territory for Plath: "I picked it not only because I know nothing, about it, but because I'll have a chance to read a great deal in philosophy and ethics ..." (*Letters Home,* 186) This course started with Aristotle and ended with D.H. Lawrence, already a favorite author of Plath's.

She lived at Whitstead, a graduate students' residence full of fellow foreigners, in a room on the third floor with a window-sofa and a gas fireplace. She explored Cambridge and found it very pleasing and quaint; from the magnificence of the King's College Chapel and the many formal gardens to "the Backs, where countless punts, canoes and scows were pushing up and down the narrow river Cam ..." (*Letters Home,* 183) But the atmosphere at Cambridge was chilly. Her room was so cold that in the morning Sylvia could see her breath in the air; butter and milk could be kept in her room without the use of a refrigerator. This amused her at first, but the legendary cold weather of Cambridge was yet to come.

As she got used to daily life, Plath noticed that women were in the distinct minority at Cambridge. Her social life soon picked up, as she decided to survey what Cambridge had to offer in her first semester. The list of local, social options was mind-boggling; she eventually decided to try out for the Amateur Dramatic Club (A.D.C.) and to attend a Labour Party Dance. Due to stress and homesickness Plath quickly suffered from a cold. After recovering she began fielding offers from Cambridge's many suitors. At the dance she met Mallory Wober, a student of Natural Sciences; they became friends immediately, and he invited her to his 'digs' (room), where he had a piano and liked to play Bach and Scarlatti. At the A.D.C., Plath tried out and was accepted to join the club. She was given the role of Phoebe Clinkett, "a verbose niece who has high-flown and very funny ambitions to write plays and poetry" (*Letters Home,* 189) in John Gay's farce, *Three Hours After Marriage.* She even saw Queen Elizabeth II and the Duke of Edinburgh at Newnham when they came to tour Cambridge.

While she was enjoying working in the theater and making new friends Plath was eager to make some progress in her writing. Unlike Smith, she had no courses in creative writing, no professor to help her in poetry or prose. In October 1955, she was too busy to even think about it, as she was still getting used to the academic and social life she had chosen. She continued to see various men, but her favorite was Wober. He was tall, good-looking, and Jewish, all qualities she admired. She was still attached romantically to Sassoon, however, and did not find anyone to replace him at Cambridge in 1955.

At Whitstead, she knew only a few other residents and got to be friendly with one, an American, Jane Baltzell, who was also reading English. Her memoir of Plath at this time, "Gone, Very Gone Youth" describes Plath as someone who "[strived] (I choose the word with care) to excel. During the first year I knew her she variously pursued horseback riding, sketching, and amateur dramatics, as well as, always, poetry. Every one of these things she did *hard,* not so much giving herself pleasure as somehow trying (so it seemed) to satisfy someone very difficult to please." (Butscher, ed., 62) This striving effort, long ago a learned habit, did not fit the Cambridge system. As Clarissa Roche, a friend of Plath's in later years, remarked in *Voices & Visions,* "I should think Sylvia was astonished to discover the difference between a woman's college in the States and a woman's college in Cambridge—utterly astonished. Whoever she was, how often she was published ... it wouldn't have meant anything [in England], they don't have stars at Oxford and Cambridge." (*Voices & Visions*)

Baltzell also remembers the ridicule Plath unwittingly caused in others due to her enthusiasm and, once, her ability to reply in kind. One morning during breakfast at Whitstead, as Plath was busy cutting up her fried eggs, another student shrilly asked, "*Must* you cut up your eggs like that?" "Sylvia and the girl eyed each other ... Sylvia cool and unruffled, somehow *pleased* ... said, 'Yes, I'm afraid I really must. What do you do with your eggs? SWALLOW THEM WHOLE?'" (Butscher, ed., 64) This anecdote points to, among other things, Plath's shortage of any real female friends while first at Cambridge. As she adjusted to English mannerisms she socialized almost exclusively with men, finding English girls to be awkward; while she considered the girls intelligent, she also thought them to be socially inferior. (*Letters Home*, 207) Plath felt that Baltzell was her closest friend, but that this friendship was tainted by rivalry.

By December 1955, Plath had decided to quit the A.D.C.; as much as she enjoyed acting and being part of a large group of creative people, she needed to write. She had already befriended fellow Cambridge student Nathaniel LaMar, who had his short story, "Creole Love Song" published in *The Atlantic Monthly*, and she had submitted some poems and short stories to Cambridge's main literary magazine, *Chequer*. They accepted two poems, "Epitaph in Three Parts" and "'Three Caryatids Without a Portic' by Hugh Robus: A Study in Sculptural Dimensions." These were her first publications in England. Her two goals now were having her Fulbright scholarship renewed and seeing Sassoon in Paris during the Christmas break. Her relationship with Mallory Wober was close enough that she was invited to stay at his family's house in London for a few days; she did stop by for a visit and was intrigued to be a Christian girl received by a Jewish family.

Just after the first semester ended, Dick Wertz, Sassoon's roommate from Yale, visited Plath in Cambridge. They went horseback riding to see the town. Plath had never ridden a horse before. Her horse, Sam, was reported as being docile but something startled him and he took off in a gallop through the busy Cambridge streets. She lost her own handle on the horse and hugged its neck for dear life. The event ended peacefully though, with Plath being shaken up and suffering only bruises. In 1959 she would write a poem about her ride on Sam, "Whiteness I Remember," but the ride itself would also stand as a moment of ecstasy for her.

Soon after she went on to meet Sassoon and took a night train with him to Nice, in the south of France. Her account of this trip in her journal is more than reminiscent of her later *Ariel* writing with its motion and color:

> France runs past. Secret, hidden, giving only the moon, rocky hills now, with clotted patches of whiteness, perhaps snow ... Then, lifting my head sleepily once, suddenly the moon shining incredibly on water. Marseille. The Mediterranean ... Sleep again, and at last the pink *vin rosé* light of dawn along the back of the hills in a strange country. Red earth ... and the blast, the blue blast of the sea on the right. The Cote d'Azur. A new country, a new year ... and the red sun rising like the eye of God out of a screaming blue sea. (*Journals*, 549)

While in the south of France, she and Sassoon took a day trip and visited the Chapelle du Rosaire nearby in Vence.[1] It was designed and decorated by Henri Matisse and she had longed to see it for years. The chapel was closed, but this did not deter her. She walked around the chapel, looking for a view to sketch. Finished, she walked around to the front and stood in front of the locked gate. A peasant told her a story of how rich people sought admittance everyday, but the church was opened only two days a week. The colors of the stained glass windows and those of southern France mixed so beautifully that she began to cry. A nun saw her and begged her not to cry, offering her entry in the chapel. Inside, she sat and thanked the nun for her kindness. (*Letters Home*, 205)

Having enjoyed seeing many different landscapes in France with Sassoon, Plath returned to Cambridge by January 10, 1956. She felt rested and ready to write and study, and felt at home back at Whitstead. She returned unsure of her standing with Sassoon, and later in the month he asked her not to write him until he contacted her. She also realized that her sensibility was more French than English; she was already studying French while at Cambridge, but vowed to work on it more. She was determined to write about her experiences in France, in Vence in particular, for publication. Her main goal, as always, was for an acceptance in *The New Yorker*, but she admitted she would settle, eventually, for a story in the *Ladies' Home Journal*. (*Letters Home*, 208) Though it appeared she was no closer to marrying Sassoon than anyone else, Plath decided to oppose a solely academic future based on her observations of the women dons at Cambridge. Instead, she believed she was destined to be a wife, mother, and writer. Plath wanted a rich, complete life as a woman, and saw all these elements as necessary for her fulfillment.

Her joy at Cambridge was short-lived. In January, she learned that her grandmother was terminally ill; the weather was snowy and cold, causing her spirits and self-confidence to become shaky. Her two poems in *Chequer* got badly reviewed. She felt the reviewer was showing off his own smug intelligence so it did not affect her too deeply. (*Letters Home*, 213) What *did* depress her besides the weather was lack of companionship. With Sassoon gone, she felt lonely. There wasn't a student she knew who was older than her, nor any female professors that she liked personally. She had rejected everyone in favor of Sassoon, whose love she doubted. By late February, she had sold a piece on Cambridge to the *Christian Science Monitor*, but otherwise she was unsure of her writing, as well. On February 25, however, things began to change.

The weather was bitter cold. A week before, her doctor suggested she go to the college psychiatrist, Dr. Davy, which she did, telling him about her breakdown and her feelings about life at Cambridge, including those of social isolation. Returning from shopping at Market Hill, she bought a copy of a new literary magazine, *Saint Botolph's Review*, and was told about a launch party for it that night in Falcon Yard, not far from the Market.[2] She arranged a date for the night with a student at Queens' College called Hamish. She read and memorized several of the poems that

afternoon, writing to her mother later, "the poetry is really brilliant ... I must admit I feel a certain sense inferiority, because
what I have done so far seems so small, smug and *little*." (*Letters
Home*, 219) That evening, escorted by Hamish, she first dropped
by a local pub to drink in the bar. She was getting over a case of
sinusitis and was slightly drunk when they arrived at the party.
The room was full of people, some dancing to a live jazz band.
It was loud and raucous, but Plath was determined to stay and
meet Ted Hughes. His writing impressed her most of all. While
she waited to meet him, she danced for a bit with another poet
she admired, Lucas Myers, an American from Tennessee.

Accounts of the first meeting of Plath and Hughes differ
slightly. Plath wrote about it first in her journal and then later as a
story, "Stone Boy with Dolphin." It was the definitive meeting for
both Plath and Hughes, violent, erotic, and memorable:

> I started yelling again about his poems and quoting "most dear
> unscratchable diamond" and he yelled back, colossal, in a voice
> that should have come from a Pole, "You like?" and asking me if I
> wanted brandy, and me yelling yes and backing into the next
> room ... I was stamping and then he was stamping on the floor,
> and then he kissed me bang smash on the mouth and ripped my
> hairband off, my lovely red hairband scarf ... and my favorite
> silver earrings: hah, I shall keep, he barked. And when he kissed
> my neck I bit him long and hard on the cheek, and when we came
> out of the room, blood was running down his face. (*Journals*,
> 211–2)

After her encounter with Hughes, she left the party with Hamish,
climbing the black, spike-tipped gate surrounding Queens College, returning to his room to make love and arrived back at
Whitstead late that night. That afternoon she wrote in her
journal about Hughes, impatient to see him again. She was hung-
over from the night before and wanted speak to him when she
was sober. By the next day, she had written a poem, "Pursuit",
about "the dark forces of lust ... It is not bad. It is dedicated to
Ted Hughes." (*Journals*, 214)

Edward James Hughes, better known as Ted Hughes, was a rising poet. He was born at 1 Aspinall Street in Mytholmroyd, a small town close to the moors in West Yorkshire on August 17, 1930. He was the youngest son in a family of three children—he had an older brother, Gerald and sister, Olwyn. His father, William fought in the First World War in Gallipoli, and worked as a carpenter for some time afterwards. By the time Ted was seven the family moved to nearby Mexborough, where William bought a tobacconist's shop. While in Mytholmroyd, Ted Hughes spent time on the moors with Gerald, who had taught him how to identify animals and birds. Gerald liked to go out hunting and fishing. At first Hughes would retrieve what his brother caught; later he would learn how to shoot a gun himself. They never went far out on to the trackless moors, but the time they spent out hunting would make a deep impression on him. The hunting they did was not all for sport; growing up in an economically depressed area, thriftiness (a virtue his mother had taught him) meant that any game caught—a partridge or rabbit—could feed a family. In World War Two, the ability to fish or hunt was a useful skill, as food was rationed; Hughes learned to pluck and draw what he and his brother caught.

In Mexborough, Hughes excelled in English. By 1944, he had started to write poems about his experiences hunting and trapping. At first inspired by Kipling's poems and novel, *The Jungle Book,* he also admired Longfellow's *Hiawatha* and parts of the Bible, including Ecclesiastes, the Song of Songs, and the Book of Job. By the end of the year, he decided he wanted to be a poet and began to seek out other writers to imitate and memorize. This was unusual for a fourteen-year-old, but as Elaine Feinstein writes: "a boy who grew up in [West Yorkshire] would be expected to demonstrate some prowess in games ... Ted, however, took no interest, although he did excel at throwing the discus, in which he competed in inter-school sports, barefooted like the Greeks. His size and craggy good looks, alongside a mischievous lack of shyness with girls ruled out any danger of his being thought effeminate." (Feinstein, 17)

Hughes did very well in school; upon graduating in 1948, he was accepted by Pembroke College in Cambridge. This did not happen very often in a place like Mexborough; only recently had students from modest backgrounds won the right to apply to elite universities like Oxford and Cambridge. After serving time as a radio operator with the RAF, Hughes went to Cambridge in the fall of 1951. He read English, but struggled; he didn't like having to write a paper every week, dissecting and criticizing writers he didn't enjoy reading. He switched his major to Social Anthropology in his third year, after having a dream. In the dream he was writing another hated essay, when a fox entered the room:

> I saw that its body and limbs had just stepped out of a furnace. Every inch was roasted, smouldering, black-charred, split and bleeding. Its eyes, which were level with mine where I sat, dazzled with the intensity of the pain. It came up and stood beside me. Then it spread its hand—a human hand as I now saw, but burned and bleeding like the rest of him—flat palm down on the blank space of my page. At the same time it said 'Stop this—you are destroying us.' (Wagner, 34)

For Ted, following instincts and intuition was part of his nature. He had grown up in a Methodist household, but also one interested in the occult. He gradually made more friends at Cambridge, other outsiders who were also poets, such as Daniel Huws, Lucas Myers, Daniel Weissbort, and Peter Redgrove. They shared a common interest in Yeats' folktales and ballads, and Robert Graves's *The White Goddess*, a poetic history of Celtic mythology. As a group they rebelled against the more moderate and polished work of the new 'Movement' poets, personified by Philip Larkin.

After Hughes graduated from Cambridge, he did various odd jobs, including working as a gardener, night watchman, and dishwasher. He lived for a while with Lucas Myers behind the St. Botolph's rectory, where he had time to read and write, but he went back to London in the fall of 1955, to work as a reader for a film company. He missed his friends and would go back to Cambridge whenever he could, usually on the weekends. He had been publishing in the magazines there, such as *Chequer* and *Granta*, and liked to read in the library and then meet his friends at their favorite pub, The Anchor. The Anchor was centrally located, adjacent to Queens' College, down the road from the St. Botolph's rectory, on the River Cam and overlooking meadows. By late February 1956, his work, along with that of Lucas Myers, Daniel Huws, and others, was published in the *Saint Botolph's Review*, edited by David Ross, another in the circle. This group knew of Plath, and her poems in *Chequer* and background in American magazines did not impress them. Lucas Myers recalled: "We disapproved of the poems in spite of their being well made, or rather partly because of it. Her ambition shined through them, or so we thought, and we thought it was not legitimate to write poetry, which should come down on the poet from somewhere, out of sheer will. Only Ted hadn't commented." (Stevenson, 312) Plath bought her copy of the *Saint Botolph's Review* from Bert Wyatt-Brown and asked if she could get an invitation to the party; it was an informal party, he said, so she wouldn't need an invitation.

Despite her intense, immediate reaction to Hughes, Plath was still in love with Sassoon. Even though Sassoon had tried to discourage her feelings for him after their Christmas holiday, Plath continued to care for him. Nevertheless, "Pursuit" was dedicated to Hughes and its epigraph is from Racine's *Phedré: Dans le fond des forets votre image me suit*—in the depths of the forest, your image pursues me. (*Letters Home*, 222–23) It is a highly charged poem, forecasting the writer's own demise at the hand of a panther. (*Collected Poems*, 22) Plath associated Hughes with the animal based on the poems she read in the *Saint Botolph's Review*.

On March 6, she received a letter from Sassoon stating he was joining the United States Army for two years and only after would then be able to start a family. Plath felt burdened by the love she had for him and in March, after having learned that her Fulbright was renewed, she went to Paris, but not before stopping in London to see Hughes. In Paris, she reached Sassoon's apartment, but he was not there. She found a pile of unopened letters she had sent him instead, and sat and wrote him another one. She then managed to see the city, going where they had gone before, sketching and writing. She sent Hughes a postcard of Rousseau's "The Snake Charmer," which she saw in Paris at the Musée d'Orsay, and he sent her two letters, which she collected at a Parisian American Express office. In early April, she met up with Gordon Lameyer and they went through Germany together; but, by the time they reached Rome, they had been fighting so much that Plath left, returning to London, and to Hughes, on April 13.

Immediately she started to write poetry and read what Hughes read, some of which she already knew: Hopkins, Yeats, Blake, Thomas, Donne, and Shakespeare. Plath's enthusiasm for Hughes was overwhelming, and her energy soared. She reveled in her ability to write, to study Plato with her favorite woman professor, Dr. Dorothea Krook, and to learn from Hughes all she could, whether it was animals, plants, or astrology—Hughes's world was all new to her. Between April and May, Plath appeared as a journalist in the Cambridge newspaper *Varsity* three times. She wrote two articles, "An American in Paris" based on her recent escapade and "Smith College in Retrospect," a look back at her college with her recent experiences at Cambridge in mind. Plath appeared as a model, as well as the writer, in the article, "May Week Fashions," wearing a bathing suit and two evening gowns, while forecasting what clothes the girls of Cambridge should wear that season.[3]

By April 29, she wrote her mother: "I have written the seven best poems of my life which make the rest look like baby-talk. I am learning and mastering new words each day ... Ted reads in his strong voice; is my best critic, as I am his." (*Letters Home,* 243) On the same day, her grandmother died, and Plath tried to comfort her mother as best she could. Plath wrote letter after letter to her mother lauding Hughes, and urged her to come visit her and meet him. Plath and Hughes were married secretly on June 16, 1956, at St. George-the-Martyr at Queen Square in London, with Aurelia as the only family member in attendance. Sylvia wanted it to remain a secret, as she was worried she would lose her Fulbright if she were married.

Each had a life-altering impact on the other. Hughes planned to go to Spain or Australia. Plath, still early in her Fulbright, planned to travel and teach. Now, Plath was writing more and, convinced of Hughes' greatness, began to type his poems and send them to American magazines. He appointed her as his agent and typist, two jobs she was more than happy to do. Her years of experience in marketing her own work were helpful for her husband's work.

The couple honeymooned in Benidorm and Alicante, Spain, visiting Paris and stopping by Madrid on the way. Once set up in Benidorm, they had a regular schedule of writing, reading, and shopping. She wrote poems and worked on stories for women's magazines, while he worked on animal fables. Later Plath wrote up her experiences of Spain in her journals, from the open markets to bullfights to their simple kitchen, for a future article in the *Christian Science Monitor*. Apart from Sylvia having a bad fever and the couple having a fight, the honeymoon went well and they returned to England in late August. On their way, they stopped off in Paris so they could meet Warren, and also at Heptonstall, in Yorkshire, so Sylvia could meet Ted's family and have somewhere to stay before her classes commenced. The Hughes' house, the Beacon, was near the moors, a few miles away from Haworth, home of the Brontë sisters. The couple hiked out to see the Brontë parsonage and Sylvia fell in love with the landscape: "I never thought I could like any country as well as the ocean, but these moors are really even better, with the great luminous emerald lights changing always, and the animals and wildness." (*Letters Home*, 270) Nearby to Heptonstall, is Hardcastle Crags, a deep, wooded valley with rocky outcroppings; this site became a poetry subject for Plath.

By October 2, Plath returned to Cambridge and found she had sold six poems to *Poetry* magazine, all new ones that she had written after meeting Hughes. She also heard from her friend, Peter Davison at *The Atlantic Monthly*, that they were publishing "Pursuit," and he was encouraging her to write a novel. Plath was happy, but found being by herself difficult, especially writing and studying. "Away from Ted, I feel as if I were living with one eyelash of myself only. It is really agony." (*Letters Home*, 276) Hughes missed his wife just as much, and they decided she should tell the authorities about their marriage. She was worried, but as it turned out, the Fulbright committee was pleased in her work and in her marriage to Hughes; Plath's tutor chided her for not telling her about the wedding earlier and allowed Plath to stay at Whitstead until the end of term.

In November Hughes moved in to a small flat at 55 Eltisley Avenue in Cambridge, and Plath joined him the next month. Through all of this she continued to write poetry and typed forty poems by Hughes for *Harper's* poetry contest, judged by Stephen Spender, Marianne Moore, and W.H. Auden—all poets Plath had met. Plath entered a similar contest for her manuscript, *Two Lovers and a Beachcomber by the Real Sea*, for the Yale Younger Poets prize at the same time. Hughes got a job teaching teenagers at a day school, and Plath continued with lectures and reading, in preparation for her exams in June. She began writing to various colleges in the States for possible teaching jobs; it was something that she felt she had to do and had found no openings so far. In late January 1957, Mary Ellen Chase came to Cambridge to see Plath and advised her to apply to Smith. With this new goal in mind, Plath also hoped to see Hughes teaching as well. (*Letters Home*, 292) Often enough Plath took the advice of her peers, which helped keep her focused. She had many alternatives racing through her head at any given time, and the guidance seemed to be always in her best interest.

On February 23, just before the first anniversary of their meeting, Ted received a telegram saying he had won the *Harper's* contest; there was no prize money, but publication of the book, *The Hawk in the Rain*, was a cause of joy for both. Plath wrote in her journal: "I am so glad Ted is first. All my pat theories against marrying a writer dissolve with Ted: his rejections more than double my sorrow and his acceptances rejoice me more than mine." (*Journals*, 271) When, a few days later, Plath was offered a job teaching at Smith, they rejoiced again.

Also that month, the new quarterly, *Gemini,* published two of Plath's poems, "Spinster" and "Vanity Fair." "Spinster," a poem about a woman who withdraws from springtime's slovenliness and fertility, was briefly reviewed in the London *Sunday Times* by their august theater critic, Harold Hobson: "Here, sharp-edged, memorable, precise, is a statement of the refusal of love, a firm, alarmed withdrawal of the skirts from the dangerous dews." (*Letters Home,* 302) Plath was pleased, especially as Hobson said he read it twelve times. She was equally pleased in April when John Lehmann, editor of the prestigious *London Magazine,* accepted "Spinster" and "Black Rook in Rainy Weather."

Davison's suggestion of a novel was one Plath followed eagerly. Aurelia's gift to the newlyweds upon their arrival in America was seven weeks at a cottage in Eastham, Cape Cod, and Plath looked forward to having the time to write without distraction. In May, she was in the midst of studying for her exams, called tripos, from morning to night. She was already plotting out her novel, which would be about an American girl in England discovering her true self. She knew she had to write something based on her own experiences, and also that she had to detach herself enough to be truthful, at the expense of people she knew. (*Letters Home,* 311) In addition to her exams, Plath also submitted a manuscript titled *Two Lovers and a Beachcomber,* containing twenty-two poems. Before leaving the university she neglected to collect her manuscript, resulting in its lying unknown for over a decade.[4] She would hold onto only five of the poems for her first collection of poetry. In late May, she wrote her exams and in the end her final mark was II-I, or B+. Packed and ready to go, Plath was more than prepared to leave: "We counted days till now all through the long, dingy winter, and America looks like the Promised Land. Both of us are delighted to leave the mean, mealy-mouthed literary world of England." (*Letters Home,* 317) As a first anniversary present, along with a large vase of pink roses, Ted dedicated *The Hawk in the Rain* to her. A few days later, they sailed to America.

# CHAPTER FIVE

# Explorations in America

*But our minds soon became two parts of one opera-*
*tion. We dreamed a lot of shared or complementary*
*dreams. Our telepathy was intrusive . . . .*

—Ted Hughes, *Paris Review*

PLATH LOOKS RADIANT IN a photograph Hughes took of her as they sailed into New York harbor on June 25, 1957. The voyage on the ocean liner *Queen Elizabeth*, from Southampton to New York, took roughly one week. As the liner docked on Manhattan's Hudson River, it marked the first time Hughes saw America and the homecoming for Plath. Although Hughes lived and worked in London for a time, Plath hoped he would feel comfortable in the United States; they did not stay in New York City for very long.

The Hughes's arrived in Wellesley on June 29, and rather than have a second wedding, Aurelia held a catered reception for over seventy family members and friends in their backyard. The wedding present Aurelia gave to her daughter and son-in-law included a seven-week stay at a cottage in Eastham, Cape Cod, Massachusetts. They stayed at Elmwood Road for a couple of weeks before being driven in mid-July to Eastham by Warren Plath, himself the recent recipient of a Fulbright. The prospect of a writing vacation pleased the newlyweds. They would entertain the occasional visitor, but they enjoyed the quiet, peaceful beach life.

The cottage at Hidden Acres, then located in the vicinity of McKoy and Pilot Roads, was a short distance from Nauset Light and Coast Guard beaches. Plath immediately began writing in her journal, setting down story ideas and motivating herself to be industrious. Her story, "All the Dead Dears," as well as a book review, was published in the summer issue of *Gemini*. In addition to thoroughly enjoying the sun, Plath also reveled in Hughes' love and presence. With the Smith school year only two months away, Plath also intended to read many novels in order to prepare for her courses; she had the freedom to decide which ones she would teach. The first author she read was Virginia Woolf, whom she greatly admired: "Her novels make mine possible: I find myself describing episodes: you don't have to follow your Judith Greenwood to breakfast, lunch, dinner ... unless the flash forwards her, reveals her. Make her enigmatic: who is that blond girl: she is a bitch: she is the white goddess. Make her a statement of the generation. Which is you." (*Journals*, 289)

Plath and Hughes explored their immediate surroundings in Eastham. Perhaps their most memorable experience came late in their vacation on August 20, when they visited Rock Harbor, a calm, low-watered cove five miles from their summer cottage, on the bay side of Cape Cod. Plath was impressed by the fiddler crabs' shyness and swiftness. She wrote in her journal about "... the drying clustered musselshells [*sic*], like some crustaceous bulbs among the tussocks. An image: weird, of another world, with its own queer habits, of mud, lumped, under-peopled with quiet crabs." (*Journals*, 297) Although the experience was memorable, it would gestate for nearly a year before becoming a poem.

She had a difficult time getting back into writing that summer; Plath was starting to sense what she *wanted* to write, but could not figure out *how* to do it. Plath claimed it had been five years since she last published a short story, but in fact she published "The Day Mr. Prescott Died" and "The Wishing Box" in Cambridge's *Granta* in October 1956 and January 1957. By July 21, she was deep into writing her short story, "The Trouble-Making Mother," and sent it for consideration to the *Saturday Evening Post*. She also wanted to publish in magazines such as *McCalls, Ladies' Home Journal, Good Housekeeping,* and *Woman's Day. (Journals,* 291) When her poetry manuscript, *Two Lovers and a Beachcomber* lost the Yale Younger Poets prize, she hit her nadir, aware that she had not worked nearly hard enough. Plath also attempted a verse play, "Dialogue Over a Ouija Board," incorporating a difficult "[seven]-line stanzas rhyming *ababcbc.*" (*Letters Home,* 324) Plath may not have done as much writing on the Cape as she had hoped, but she was getting closer to what she wanted with Hughes' support. On August 21, she wrote: "But be honest. No more mother's helper stories with phony plots. It wasn't all phony, but slicked over, without the quirks, to move fast. And Ted will be proud of me, which is what I want. He doesn't care about the flashy success, but about me [and] my writing. Which will see me through." (*Journals,* 296)

In September, the Hughes's moved to Northampton. They rented a third floor rear apartment at 337 Elm Street, a mile from Smith College and next to Child's Memorial Park. It was not large, but after their grisly living conditions in Cambridge, it was passable. The apartment was mostly furnished, so they only needed to add a desk and shelves for their books. As the semester drew closer, Plath became insecure about her qualifications for teaching. Her teaching schedule included classes on most days, including Saturday, and three hours in her office where students could drop by for scheduled appointments. She taught her classes in Seelye Hall, located in-between College Hall and the Nielson library. As an instructor of freshman English, Plath would lead discussions, rather than hold lectures. In addition to her course load, she helped Newton Arvin, formerly one of her professors, grade papers for money, which necessitated rereading her favorite authors such as Nathaniel Hawthorne, Henry James, and Herman Melville. (*Journals,* 319–22) She told her mother that she prepared for her classes by "[preparing] the main points to cover and perhaps a little background material." (*Letters Home,* 327) She was restless and sleepless before her first day of classes.

The fall brought the publication of *The Hawk in the Rain,* the first and highly esteemed collection of poetry by Hughes, who gave his first poetry reading in the United States in New York on October 20, accompanied by Plath. (Burroway, 117) One of the more glorious reviews that ran in the *New York Times Book Review* was by the American poet W. S. Merwin, who would eventually befriend the Hughes's. Merwin lived with his wife, Dido, in Beacon Hill at the time; his review of *The Hawk in the Rain* appeared on October 6, 1957. (Stevenson, 117)

On October 1, Plath wrote herself a letter she called "Letter to a demon." She had been teaching for less than a week, but already she was feeling that she was a failure. She was most worried that she was letting down people like Mary Ellen Chase and Alfred Young Fisher, two of the Smith faculty members who had encouraged her to apply for the position. By writing down the details of her paranoia in the form of a letter, something she first did in the summer of 1953, she was able to be objective regarding her situation. The demon she addresses is that part of her which caused the suicide attempt four years earlier. Plath tried hard to control her demon, and, because she knew she was unhappy, she worked to bring her spirits back up. One way of changing her mood was to construct a schedule for writing. She conceded she was not an experienced teacher and commanded herself to be patient, admitting "not being perfect hurts." (*Journals*, 620) Plath was dedicated to her journal and the advice she gave herself was genuine and beneficial. Teaching at Smith took up all her energy: preparing for her classes, attending staff meetings, holding office hours, and faculty socializing during the fall took its toll on Plath. She often found herself unable to write.

She decided to set goals each week, no matter how small, in order to improve her confidence. The pressure she imposed on herself to write poems, stories, and a novel was excessively demanding. In early November, Plath wrote a letter to her brother describing many of the issues she had with teaching. One of her fiercest concerns was being seen as a successful Smith student, who returned as a mediocre or even bad teacher. The interference on her writing caused by the rigors of teaching was made clear: "How I long to write on my own again! When I'm describing Henry

James' use of metaphor to make emotional states vivid and concrete, I'm dying to be making up my own metaphors." (*Letters Home,* 330) Plath had many papers to grade by the end of the semester. She had sixty-five students, and it took much dedication to maintain the appropriate mindset for teaching. Plath was asked back unofficially to teach another year by the end of the month, so her fears of inadequacy were temporarily laid to rest. (*Letters Home,* 331)

Regardless of being asked back to teach, it was clear that Plath could not stay; Hughes was also finding it difficult to write. They made tentative plans to leave Northampton in favor of Boston at the end of the spring semester. In order to reach this goal, they needed more income. Aside from Plath's wages as a teacher, the couple was earning only a modest income as writers. The solution was clear: Hughes needed to find employment. He began to look for a job in December, with no luck at first, and then searched beyond Northampton. After classes ended for the semester, Plath came down with viral pneumonia, which was complicated by physical exhaustion. They spent the Christmas holiday at the family home in Wellesley. Though she was tired, Plath could look back on 1957 as a successful year: she had published more than 20 poems in England and the United States.

Once back in Northampton, Plath was determined to make the most of her job. She started by trying to get along better with her students; yet, she could not help feeling ostracized by the faculty members and was tired of hosting them as guests. Her classes were better; she particularly enjoyed her middle class, taught at eleven in the morning. To make extra money, she offered to grade Newton Arvin's exams. She was writing a little, putting the finishing touches on a children's story about kitchen gadgets that change responsibilities.[1] Hughes found a job teaching at the University of Massachusetts at Amherst, a short drive away. They also began to consider moving to Boston in the spring, planning to apartment hunt in March or April. Boston would provide more material for their writing; Plath was anxious to know Boston, its streets, and people. In her journal, she knew where to start: "Rooms. Every room a world. To be god: to be every life before we die: a dream to drive men mad. But to be one person, one woman—to live ... learn others lives and make them into print ... " (*Journals,* 306) In early February 1958, Plath received a letter from *Art News,* a magazine based in New York City, commissioning her to write a poem inspired by a work of art. She immediately thought of Gauguin and Rousseau, artists whose work she had admired for years. (*Journals,* 332)

Plath started to work on her poem for *Art News* immediately. The right poem was slow to form and it took her until mid-March to finally hit on the right concept. Plath admitted in her journal that she and Hughes had very few friends in Northampton, but she felt comfortable enough with the few they had. (*Journals,* 326) The Hughes befriended Plath's fellow English instructor, Paul Roche and his wife, Clarissa, during the school year, and they all spent a number of evenings together. Although Plath and Hughes both found Northampton lacked the right social atmosphere, they were successful in making lifelong friends that year. Anther important friendship they made during that year was with Esther and Leonard Baskin. Leonard was one of America's preeminent artists and sculptors; he taught at Smith for over two decades and in later years collaborated with Hughes on several books of poetry.

As Plath contemplated the art poems, she was still working on putting a book together from her Cambridge poems. By late February, she titled the book, *The Earthenware Head,* taken from her 1957 poem, "The Lady and the Earthenware Head." Cyrilly Abels accepted poems by both Plath ("November Graveyard") and Hughes ("Pennines in April") in late February. Plath recorded in her journal that it was her "first acceptance for about a year." (*Journals,* 338) This singular acceptance catapulted Plath into her most prolific writing period to date.

Over the Smith spring break in March, Plath wrote eight poems in eight days, taking full advantage of her free time. She found inspiration not only in Gauguin and Rousseau, but also in the surreal works of the Italian painter, Giorgio de Chirico. "On the Decline of Oracles" and "The Disquieting Muses" are two poems based on de Chirico's paintings; she also wrote a sestina on Rousseau's "The Dream" which she titled "Yadwigha, On a Red

Couch, Among Lilies: A Sestina for the Douanier." Rousseau also provided inspiration for her poem, "Snakecharmer." Plath wrote four poems based on Paul Klee: "Virgin in a Tree," "Perseus: The Triumph of Wit Over Suffering," "Battle-Scene: From the Comic Operatic Fantasy *The Seafarer*," and "The Ghost's Leavetaking." In all, the poems represent a breakthrough for Plath. She wrote intensely and, though none of the poems are known to have appeared in *Art News*, her reward was proof that she could still write poetry. Plath was so pleased with her poems she thought herself fit to be "The Poetess of America" and believed Ted "[would] be The Poet of England and her dominions." (*Journals*, 360)

With less than eight weeks remaining in the semester, Plath begrudgingly performed her duties. Her main concern about leaving Smith was that she had let down her supporters. She was also paranoid that her colleagues were talking about her behind her back. Her classes still needed preparation, and she planned to teach W. B. Yeats, Dylan Thomas, Gerald Manley Hopkins, T.S. Eliot, John Crowe Ransom, E.E. Cummings, and W. H. Auden— all poets she admired as an undergraduate. Plath was trying to write poems as well, but she was temporarily stalled because she was waiting to hear if *The New Yorker* would accept any of the poems she sent to them. By early April, she was again sick with a sinus infection, which left her exhausted and practically bedridden. Plath went back to Wellesley in mid-April so she could visit a city doctor and also because Hughes was giving a reading at Harvard. The reading was well attended and, although Plath was still sick, she enjoyed meeting Adrienne Rich and spending the evening having dinner at Felicia's, an Italian restaurant in Boston's North End.[2] The highlight of the evening took place when Jack Sweeney, a professor of English at Harvard, asked Plath to record some of her poems for the Woodberry Poetry Room at Harvard. Prior to that, on April 18, Plath recorded a dozen poems, including several of her art poems, in Springfield, Massachusetts with Lee Anderson. A copy was also deposited at the Library of Congress in Washington, D.C.

The art poems Plath had written excited her and she was eager to keep writing. Within a few months, she wrote many more poems, each bettering a previous one. Poems such as "Sculptor," "Lorelei," and "Full Fathom Five" broke open a source of poetry previously unknown to her. When Plath wrote "Mussel Hunter at Rock Harbor," she not only wrote one of her longest poems, but had also taken observations directly from a journal entry and set it to poetry. Many of the same words from the journal entry appeared in the poems: "queer," "grass-root," and "mud." Plath struck at the living grass roots of Rock Harbor and, ninety-one lines later, she had a poem better than nearly all her previous works.

Tensions began to mount in early May. Perhaps this was due to some uncertainty in their future regarding their imminent departure from the academic life and beginning to write full-time. One incident involved Hughes accusing Plath of discarding some of his belongings and Plath denying the accusation. Plath left the apartment and returned shortly only to find Hughes had left the apartment. She then "sat in the park—all vast, dark, ominously full of silent Teds [*sic*], or no Ted," before she finally found him. (*Journals*, 372) As the last day of Plath's year at Smith approached, she became anxious and excited to celebrate her freedom from teaching. Plath had been in school since she was a child in Winthrop and, after more than twenty years in various educational systems, she was calling it quits in order to write. On May 6, Plath attended a poetry reading by Robert Lowell. Upon reading his poems she had "oddly a similar reaction (excitement, joy, admiration, curiosity to meet [and] praise) as when I first read Ted's poems ..." (*Journals*, 379)

On May 21 and 22, the tensions between Plath and Hughes came to a climax in two separate incidents. Hughes had agreed to participate in a reading of *Oedipus the King* with Paul Roche and several other Smith faculty members held at Sage Hall. He explicitly requested that Plath not attend. (*Journals*, 387) But, she defied this request and raced to the hall, trying to sneak into the performance without his noticing from the stage. Her attempt to remain invisible failed, though. As she tried to calm herself from running, she wrote, "the minute I came in he knew it, and I knew he knew it ... He was ashamed of something." (*Journals*, 388) What Plath was not immediately aware of was Hughes's embarrassment and lack of enthusiasm at his role in the production. The next day, Plath's last day of classes, she and Hughes decided to meet immediately after her last class to celebrate. They drove to the campus together and agreed to meet at their car after her final class released. The day went well; Plath received applause from all her students. Plath ran to the parking lot after her last class expecting to see her husband in their car; but he was not there. She then drove to the library, but he was nowhere to be seen. Intuitively, Plath walked toward Paradise Pond, taking a path that ran between the Library and Haven House, where she saw her husband and a female student "coming up the road from Paradise Pond where the girls take their boys to neck on weekends." (*Journals*, 390) Furious, Plath paced toward them but the girl ran off. Later that week a physical fight ensued; scars branded the couple for the second time.[3]

In June, after she and Hughes had reconciled, Plath wrote "Child's Park Stones," a loving description of their neighboring park in Northampton. Her inspiration from local atmosphere would be magnified in Boston, where rich history and culture would be at their doorstep. By June 20, they hoped to rent a small, sixth-floor apartment with a view of the Charles River at 9 Willow Street on Beacon Hill.

By now, Plath was writing most of her poems using a syllabic form.[4] Syllabics, as she explained to her brother in a letter dated June 11, 1958, "[measures] lines not by heavy and light stresses, but by the *number* of syllables." (*Letters Home,* 344) "Mussel Hunter at Rock Harbor," (a poem she included in this letter) written in this style, has seven syllables per line. On June 25, after having been rejected at *The New Yorker* for many years, Plath finally received a letter of acceptance from Howard Moss for two recent poems: "Mussel Hunter at Rock Harbor" and "Nocturne."[5] Plath was ecstatic, writing in her journal: "I ran yipping upstairs to Ted ... this shot of joy conquers an old dragon & should see me through the next months of writing on the crest of a creative wave." (*Journals,* 397)

This joy did not last long. At various times during their first year in the United States, Plath endured writing blocks, and soon after *The New Yorker* acceptance, she had another one. When she was unable to produce on the page, she turned to her journal. There she wrote: "Prose writing had become a phobia to me: my mind shuts [and] I clench." (*Journals*, 403) Later she wrote, "Vague aims—to write—fall stillborn." (*Journals*, 409) In early July, they brought out their ouija board and spoke with their spirit, Pan, whose god is "Kolossus"; Pan told her to write about the Lorelei.[6] As a result, Plath wrote a poem, "Lorelei," which explored her Germanic roots. She also wrote what she considered to be a book poem called "Whiteness I Remember," about her runaway horse, Sam, from Cambridge. "Mussel Hunter at Rock Harbor" appeared in the August 9, 1958 issue of *The New Yorker*. Plath was ecstatic at seeing her poem, and name, on the famous *New Yorker* font. Also that week, the *Christian Science Monitor* published her illustrated article, "Beach Plum Season on Cape Cod." Plath's skill for drawing never diminished. In fact, her eye for detail infused all her work.

As their year in Northampton came to a close, Boston brought the promise of a new beginning. Beacon Hill has always been a place for poets. 9 Willow Street is perpendicular to and overlooks the beautiful, cobbled Acorn Street, and steps away from Louisburg Square, both considered among the most exclusive streets in the United States.[7] Plath struggled to write even as she got reacquainted with Boston. She enjoyed Scollay Square's tattoo parlors, bars, and burlesque theaters.[8] She took advantage of Boston's Haymarket on Blackstone Street for cheap produce. Most of Boston's attractions, including the Public Library, the Charles River, Boston Common, and the Downtown Crossing shopping district, were less than one mile from their doorstep. Plath began to worry about money and took a part-time job working at Massachusetts General Hospital typing patient records in the psychiatric department. She compiled her own set of notes from the hospital. Many of the names or symptoms appeared in later stories. Still suffering from writer's block late in 1958, Plath sought private, professional help.

On December 10, Plath started to see her former McLean psychiatrist, Dr. Ruth Beuscher. From the outset, Beuscher took the risk of giving Plath permission to hate her mother. In the eight years of letter writing, the impression is given that Plath's mother was her closest confidant, second only to her journals. Few letters were exchanged between Plath and her mother during the Boston year because they lived close enough to speak on the phone regularly. (*Letters Home*, 322) Plath called the sessions "interviews," and made copious notes after each of their discussions. The first of these are on pink Smith College memo paper. Plath also started to draft poems and other writings on this paper, which she had pilfered from the supply cabinets at Smith during the spring.[9]

Dr. Beuscher talked at length with her client about her father, husband, and life, and used Freudian psychoanalysis to help her patient. Plath exhibited symptoms of an Electra complex, which is in part defined by hostility toward the mother. She began to blame her mother for her father's untimely death and was encouraged to confront these issues through her writing. These interviews lasted into the spring and drew out some deep-seated emotions from Plath and often left her in tears. The purpose was to free Plath in order to end her writer's block, and it worked.

After several years of hard work, 1959 would mark Plath's becoming a major writer. The quality and quantity of her work increased remarkably compared to the previous few years. In January, she wrote several good poems exploring subjects scaling her life, such as "The Bull of Bendylaw" about her honeymoon and "Point Shirley" about her childhood. Previously, Plath showed signs of being inhibited about poetic subjects, struggling always to write about anything other than the present. The sessions with Dr. Beuscher encouraged Plath to look back. In February, Plath began auditing Robert Lowell's poetry seminar at Boston University. In 1959, Lowell published a pioneering collection of poetry, *Life Studies,* with subjects ranging from his own stay at McLean Hospital to his family history, and poems that were also deeply personal. It was an influential book for many younger poets, including Plath, George Starbuck, W.D. Snodgrass, and Anne Sexton.

The seminar was important to Plath; since she was only auditing the classes, there was less compulsion for perfection. Her previous poems were constrained by form and syllables. Through reading Lowell and Sexton, she began to break away from such strict writing practices. She also spent time outside of class with Sexton; they frequented the bar at the Ritz-Carlton Hotel after class to drink and discuss poetry and suicide. Sexton was a rival poet, but Plath did not treat her as one. Plath was very competitive with Adrienne Rich, but gradually that animosity would disappear. Plath wrote poems about Benidorm, Cambridge, Winthrop, and Cape Cod. She began to use location and personal narrative together, making true, sound poems. The stories Plath was writing were also gaining depth. A series of Boston-based stories, including "Johnny Panic and the Bible of Dreams," "The Daughters of Blossom Street," and "The Fifteen-Dollar Eagle" possessed a slang language and more complicated themes than her earlier ones. Plath wanted to write a novel, so several stories had consistent ideas running through them.

Plath was getting acceptance through the winter and spring, as well, which only encouraged her more. *Mademoiselle* featured Plath, Hughes, and two other poets in their January 1959 issue. The article, titled "Four Young Poets," also printed Plath's poem, "The Times are Tidy." The *Christian Science Monitor* printed two articles, featuring more of Plath's drawings in May and June. In particular, Plath's "A Walk to Withens," recalls her journey through the Yorkshire moors in search of Top Withens, the house that supposedly inspired *Wuthering Heights*. In March, Plath had even more inspiration to write when she and Hughes visited Winthrop.

About a decade had passed since Plath had been in Winthrop. Much of it may have remained the same, but Plath had changed. No longer eager to run along the beach with her friends, Plath visited her former family homes and also her father's grave. Serious discussion of her dead father was established in her interviews with Dr. Beuscher, and it may have been her suggestion that Plath visit his grave, perhaps for the first time.[10] The importance of their day trip cannot be underestimated. Plath wrote several poems in the following weeks, many on the subject of her father. In "Electra on Azalea Path," Plath blames her love for her father for his demise; in the "The Beekeeper's Daughter" she confesses feeling oppressed under his authority.

By the spring of 1959, the Hughes's were hoping for a child. Plath had an irregular menstrual cycle, leading often to confusion and false hopes.[11] On March 20, her period arrived "after a long 40 day period of hope, the old blood, cramps, and spilt fertility." (*Journals*, 474) On the same day, she wrote a playful poem titled "Metaphors." The poem has nine lines, and nine syllables per line, mirroring the nine months of pregnancy. In June, Plath went to see a doctor, who decreed that Plath was not ovulating properly. This was a serious blow to her ego; Plath felt if a woman was barren, then she was flawed in a great way. In her journal she writes, "Suddenly the deep foundations of my being are gnawn [*sic*]. I have come ... to the point where my desires and emotions and thoughts center around what the normal woman's center around, and what do I find? Barrenness." (*Journals*, 500)

In the spring, Yaddo, a writer's colony in Saratoga Springs, New York, invited Plath and Hughes to stay from September through November. Around the same time, they started having serious discussions of returning to England, where Hughes was hoping Plath would give birth to a child; Hughes had won a Guggenheim award, so they were free to live and travel where they wanted. With this in mind, Plath wanted to make a cross-country trip to California, so they could both see America before returning to England. Plath also hoped to meet her father's sister, Frieda Plath Heinrichs, who lived in Pasadena, California. They set off in early July for a ten-week vacation through Ontario, Canada, Wisconsin, the Dakotas, and Yellowstone National Park.

The experience of traveling cross-country and camping was new to Plath. At the outset of their vacation, Plath was pregnant but she did not know it. The journey was a success; the only trouble they had was a bear breaking their car window one night at Yellowstone. Plath's poem, "Two Campers in Cloud Country" remembers Rock Lake, Ontario, Canada. The poem is calm, like the water, sky, and quiet she enjoyed while there. She writes: "I lean to you ... Tell me I'm here," because she feels dwarfed by the immense sky. (*Collected Poems*, 145) Plath wrote the story, "The Fifty-Ninth Bear" after staying in Yellowstone. In the story, Sadie and Norton are counting bears, and Sadie bets Norton some money that they would see fifty-nine bears. By the end of the story, Sadie's number is met but at Norton's expense, as the fifty-ninth bear mauls him. In her journal, Plath expressed displeasure about the story in mid-September, 1959, but she still sent it out.

The Hughes's traveled through Arizona, Texas, Louisiana, Tennessee, and Washington, D.C. on their way back to Massachusetts; by the time they returned to Wellesley, Plath was nearly two months pregnant. With less than two weeks before they were expected at Yaddo in September, they finalized plans to return to England before Christmas, packed up 9 Willow Street and brought their belongings to Wellesley.

Each writer at Yaddo has a workroom, and in the Hughes's case, they shared a large bedroom. In 1959, Yaddo's prized rose garden was not open to the public, as it is today, so the artists and writers had access to a vast amount of private grounds. Her two months at Yaddo were very productive; she wrote thirteen "book" poems, including a seven-part poem titled, "Poem for a Birthday," inspired by the poems of Theodore Roethke, whom Plath was reading at the time. Her writer's block was defeated. Plath's best Yaddo poem, "The Colossus," about her dead father, muses, "I shall never get you put together entirely,/ Pieced, glued, and properly jointed." (*Collected Poems*, 129) Many of the poems reflect on her surroundings and her breakdown and recovery.

Plath found many magazines and journals interested in her 1959 poems, including the *London Magazine*, which became a faithful publisher, and *The New Yorker*, which also began accepting her more frequently. In the two and a half years spent in the United States, teaching, writing, and traveling had all been successful. Plath was noticeably pregnant by the time she returned to Boston in early November. The last poem Plath wrote in the United States, "Mushrooms," is quietly sure of itself. The mushrooms are a metaphor for Plath's writing life:

Little or nothing.
So many of us!
So many of us!

We are shelves, we are
Tables, we are meek,
We are edible ...

Our kind multiplies:

We shall by morning
Inherit the earth.
Our foot's in the door. (*Collected Poems*, 139–140)

The line, "Our kind multiplies" may be a nod to Anne Sexton's poem, "Her Kind," about women having many identities, which Plath heard during Lowell's poetry course. In 1959 she began to confront the iconic figure of her father and to write about her own feelings and experiences, and, as she and Hughes once again traveled across the Atlantic, she had high hopes for her work and her new life in London.

# CHAPTER SIX

# Confined Spaces

*Forget myself, myself. Become a vehicle of the world,*
*a tongue, a voice, Abandon my ego.*
—Sylvia Plath, *Journals*,

BEFORE SHE BECAME PREGNANT, Plath seemed ambivalent regarding children. Two years before in 1958, she railed against the American dream's pressures and expectations of getting a house, having a job, and raising children. (*Journals*, 411) Plath believed she was not ready for a baby, at least she did not want a baby until she established herself as a writer; she feared the energies involved in childrearing might lessen her compulsion to write. As her pregnancy developed and she sailed away from home for good, the significance of the recent poems Plath wrote at Yaddo was unknown. She was sure they were her best poems and began a new manuscript based on them. They spent Christmas in Yorkshire before traveling back to London in January 1960 to look for a flat. Unfortunately, there are very few existing journal entries for Plath after she returned to England.[1] The letters she wrote to her family and friends in the United States are a rich source of information, but the letters show only half of the story.

In London, W.S. Merwin and his wife, Dido, lived at 11 St. George's Terrace. Their building, the last on an ascending, dead-end block, had a commanding view of Primrose Hill, just across the busy Primrose Hill Road. Within close walking distance were the London Zoo, Regent's Park, and the markets at Camden Town. Still close after their time in Boston, the Merwins were integral in assisting the Hughes's in finding a flat and getting settled. Establishing themselves in a home was crucial as Plath was now within three months of her due date. After a stressful two weeks of looking for a flat and staying at different places, the Hughes's looked at two flats in the Merwins' neighborhood. They took a three-year lease on a small flat on the third floor at 3 Chalcot Square, just a few minutes' walking distance to the Merwins'.

After signing the lease they traveled back to Heptonstall. They spent the last two weeks of January at the Beacon packing their belongings. Plath's letters to her mother confessed to feeling tired and homesick. Those feelings soon evaporated, however, as she only needed time to settle in London. She wrote a playful poem titled, "You're" around this time. "You're" is a casual poem, much like "Mushrooms." In the poem, she imagines the baby's happiness as it twists and turns in the womb. Many of the poems she had been writing were the result of exercises Hughes had given her.[2] Compassionate about her writer's blocks, Hughes made lists of subjects for Plath's possible poems; his lists, preserved at Smith College, helped Plath formulate ideas. Habitually, Plath marked a poem idea with a star or a dot, and also wrote down the title of her poem. Some of Plath's poems inspired by these lists are "Mushrooms," "The Earthenware Head," "Winter Ship," "On Deck," "Sleep in the Mojave Desert," the series "Poem for a Birthday," and many future poems.

Plath reordered her manuscript to include the recent poems in a new volume. She continually rearranged her poems, attempting to find the right pattern for them, and removed anything she considered too old or weak; all the poems included were written after she married Hughes. It was a laborious process, but by early February 1960, she had settled on the final order of the poems, and a title, *The Colossus and Other Poems*. The title comes from the ninth poem in her arrangement, "The Colossus." It was her strongest poem and it calls attention to her best subject: the mythology of herself and her father.

During February, the Hughes's were hard at work making their flat feel like a home. The flat was almost too small to live in, but it responded gracefully to their personal tastes and improvements. One of their first purchases was a new bed. They also accepted offers for furniture and carpets from the Merwins. Because it lacked the space for a study, Hughes set up a foldaway table in the hallway by the door for his space to write. His second collection of poems, *Lupercal*, was scheduled to be published in March. The promise his first collection showed was matched and bettered in *Lupercal*. Again, Plath received the book's dedication. Faber was also going to publish a children's book by Hughes later in the year. The Hughes's decided to dedicate this book, *Meet My Folks!*, to their soon-to-be-born child. They had decided on their baby's names: Frieda Rebecca, after her recently met aunt Frieda, or Nicholas Farrar. Farrar was a Hughes family name, which dated back to 1625. (Feinstein, 5) Dido Merwin introduced Plath to her doctor, Dr. John Horder, who lived nearby at 98 Regent's Park Road, in January. She immediately liked him, and he introduced her to an obstetrician. Three midwives were assigned to her and she found them all agreeable; Plath's only choice for birth was to have a midwife assist in a home delivery, which she favored over the hospital. (*Letters Home*, 361) The Merwins not only introduced them to the right people, they were also very selfless. Sympathetic to his lack of space, the Merwins offered their study to Hughes to work in, since they would spend much of the spring and summer at their second home in France.

With her typed manuscript ready to send to English publishers, Plath was full of hope. The first publisher she sent her poems to was William Heinemann Ltd., located at 15-16 Queen Street in Mayfair. She met with James Michie, an editor at Heinemann, who had probably sent Plath a letter in October 1959, saying he was impressed by "In Midas' Country" and "The Thin People," poems that appeared in a recent issue of *London Magazine*. (*Journals*, 521) Heinemann replied to Plath within a week, accepting the manuscript. On February 10, Plath met with Michie at the York Minster pub on Dean Street in Soho. He also acted as her literary agent for American publishers, saving Plath some time and work. (*Letters Home*, 366) Plath achieved her goal of getting a book accepted for publication before she had a child. The book was slated for publication in late 1960; Plath requested it be published as close to her birthday as possible. In total, the book contained fifty poems, of which the Yaddo poems comprised one-third. The Wellesley *Townsman* ran an article on April 14, 1960, announcing the publication for the fall. Plath decided to have her maiden name appear as the author, rather than her married name, because she almost always published under her maiden name. In fact, the only known published work under the name, "Sylvia Plath Hughes," was "Cambridge Vistas," which appeared in the *Institute of International Education News Bulletin* in 1958.

As the due date for her baby approached, Plath was advised by her doctors and midwives to get more rest. In late February and early March, a string of visitors disrupted the preparations for the baby. In a letter to her mother, Plath wrote that she "really put [her] foot down about visitors now," (*Letters Home*, 368) admitting she was pleased their next guest, Olwyn, intended to stay with friends. Around mid-March, she endured a two-week sinus infection, which only frustrated her. Her spirits were slightly revived when it was announced that *The Hawk in the Rain* was the recipient of the 1960 Somerset Maugham award, a prize worth £500.[3] The money was to be used traveling outside of the United Kingdom in order to learn about other cultures and ways of life. Plath and Hughes discussed spending time in places such as Greece, the south of France, or Italy. When *Lupercal* was published in late March, it was an even greater success than Hughes's first collection. As a result of the publication, and an all-praising review by the preeminent literary critic, A. Alvarez in London's *Observer*, invitations and requests for readings and parties from all over the country poured into 3 Chalcot Square.

April was the month of Plath births: Otto, Aurelia, and Warren were all born in April. On April 1, 1960, Frieda Rebecca Hughes was born at 5:45 a.m., after a relatively short labor. Plath commented that Frieda had her nose and she felt that it looked better on the baby than it did her own face. (*Letters Home*, 374) She called her mother at their Wellesley house to share the news, even though it was still in the middle of the night. As Plath was ever eager to gain more experience in life, she was open to natural childbirth. Her doctors required that she stay in the house for ten days, requesting she do as little as possible. After this, she and Hughes adjusted to waking at night, changing diapers, and other new responsibilities.

One of Plath's first outdoor adventures with Frieda took place on Easter Sunday. Plath and her daughter, along with Peter Redgrove, also a poet, went to Trafalgar Square to witness the "Ban the Bomb" march that was entering central London. She sat just in front of the National Gallery with other mothers. Plath's political views are seldom highlighted, but she was clearly against nuclear arms.[4] Hughes had gone with Dido, earlier, to watch Merwin in the march at Hyde Park. Plath's decision to attend the rally was a surprise to Hughes, who returned home to find an empty flat. Throughout the spring there were periods of high tension with the family. From the transatlantic crossing, traveling across England, getting settled in their new home, and expecting the baby, the couple were only starting to settle down. With these events, especially the arrival of Frieda, their relationship began to change.

On April 21, as the Hughes's adjusted to parenthood, the demand for *Lupercal* was so great that a second printing was ordered in June, which led Faber to host a cocktail party. On May 4, before attending a dinner at the home of T.S. Eliot, Plath received her proof copy for *The Colossus*. The fifty poems filled eighty-eight pages; Plath wrote, "[T]he book will look handsome ... The poems are so beautifully *final.*" (*Letters Home,* 380) That night, the Hughes employed their first babysitter as they set out for the Eliots'. Plath was full of nerves. However, the evening passed cordially, and Plath was seated at dinner between Eliot and Stephen Spender. They met again in June at another Faber cocktail party, this time to celebrate W. H. Auden. A photograph of all the different Faber poets—including Eliot, Auden, Spender, Hughes and Louis MacNeice—was taken, marking the official acceptance of Hughes as a major poet. Plath, having acted as Hughes's secretary and publicist, as well as his biggest admirer, was extremely pleased to see her husband in such company.

The natural noises in the flat due to caring for the baby distracted Hughes as he tried to write, so he began to work at the Merwins' study in May. A. Alvarez visited their flat to interview Hughes for the *Observer* and visited with Plath. This was his first meeting with Plath, even though he had previously accepted her poem, "Night Shift," which had appeared in the *Observer* under the title of "Poem" on June 14, 1959.[5] Alvarez was not aware that "Sylvia Plath" and "Mrs. Ted Hughes" were one in the same. This caused some minor embarrassment but all was forgiven. (Alvarez, *Savage God*, 23–24) To have Alvarez as a contact and friend meant much in terms of professional opportunities; thus, this meeting proved to be their most important in 1960.

At the cocktail party in April, Plath met the young American novelist, Janet Burroway, who had also won a Guest Editorship at *Mademoiselle* and was currently at Cambridge on a scholarship. The two got along well, and Plath invited her and a friend to supper on May 7. Burroway recalls a moment from her visit:

> I stood in the doorway of the narrow kitchen talking with Sylvia, who held Frieda in the crook of her left arm while she rattled pots with her right ... I may have been too nervous of a five-week-old, or she may have feared Frieda would cry in a stranger's arms ... Sylvia was increasingly brittle, taut. Finally she took the baby into the living room and with some emphasis handed her to Ted—I want to say *shoved her at*. (Burroway, 15)

Burroway got the impression Plath was Frieda's main caretaker, though in fact Hughes did look after Frieda some of the time when Plath was away.

Although it was almost impossible for Plath to find time to write poetry while caring for her new baby, she did enjoy seeing her work published throughout the year. "Man in Black," "Watercolor of Grantchester Meadows," and "The Net Menders" all appeared in *The New Yorker*. *London Magazine* printed her story "The Daughters of Blossom Street" in May. Anxious to start writing again in peace and quiet, Plath began to use the Merwins' study in the morning. After a painful start, she wrote a poem in late June called, "The Hanging Man." The image first draws upon the ECT shock treatments she received during the summer of 1953. Her willingness to probe her deeper self in writing, with credit to Lowell's poetry course, was taking shape.

Hughes sold the manuscripts to his two collections of poems to a rare book dealer in London who was acting on behalf of the Lilly Library at Indiana University. They were trying to save all the money they could at this point. The flat was much too small for the family with the addition of Frieda. Plath was behind Hughes in terms of poetic assuredness, always supporting his endeavor for writing full time. They made very few plans during the summer, only to nurse Frieda and get into their own routines for house-keeping and shopping. In August, just after Ted's thirtieth birthday, they traveled to Yorkshire for a small holiday. They took an overnight visit to Whitby, on the eastern coast of North York-shire, with Ted's cousin, Victoria Farrar. Plath was not impressed by the English coast, and in particular with seaside resorts, including Whitby.[6] She was also displeased that everything was very dirty, and that even in August, people wore "woolen suits and coats and tinted plastic raincoats." (*Letters Home,* 391) At this time, Plath still wanted to become a successful story writer; she enjoyed her time in Yorkshire and anticipated writing poems and stories about her experience.

Upon returning to their small flat, the Hughes's became more serious about buying a house. Plath started writing poetry again, completing "Leaving Early," "Love Letter," "Candles," and "A Life" before the end of the year. Another major event occurred in October, when Heinemann published *The Colossus.* Plath mailed her mother and brother copies on October 26, just a day before her birthday. Reviews were slow to appear, but when they did sur-face, they were mostly positive. Alvarez all but demanded readers to take notice of Plath's work, stating that she was writing remark-able poetry, unlike any other poetess he had read. (Alvarez, *Observer,* 12) Plath was somewhat disheartened by the lack of press, but she continued to practice her craft and hone her skills.

At the same time her book was published, the obscenity trial of D.H. Lawrence's *Lady Chatterley's Lover* was taking place at the

Old Bailey in London. Lawrence died in 1930, and his novel was published secretly in 1928. It was banned in England and the United States for a time. In the novel, Lady Chatterley has an affair because her husband is not capable of having sexual intercourse.[7] The second day of the trial took place on Plath's birthday, and she was in attendance. Plath recorded the proceedings in a notebook, copying down the questions and answers posed by the judge and the witnesses. She also received a press pass for the last day of the trial, courtesy of Spender. Plath had long admired Lawrence and was excited at the verdict of not guilty: it meant the book could be published in its original edition, uncensored.[8]

Aside from the excitement of the trial, domestic items held Plath's attention as well. Frieda began teething during the autumn, which again kept her parents up during the night, leaving them feeling exhausted much of the time. As new parents, they would be better prepared to cope with their next child. Plath was looking forward to spending her third Christmas at the Beacon, and they arrived in the middle of December. Plath was hopeful about getting regular work with the British Broadcasting Corporation (BBC), as Hughes was doing. She recorded several poems, including "Candles" and "Leaving Early," and explored the possibility of doing a program about American women poets. Though Plath was achieving recognition as a poet, she still hoped to break into the short story market for women's magazines.

In November, Plath wrote her mother with news that she was writing short stories. Drafts of uncollected short stories are held in the Plath collections at Smith College, Indiana University, and Emory University.[9] Plath was also contacted by a literary agent, who had connections in New York City. The agent read a story of Plath's in the *London Magazine*, most likely "The Daughters of Blossom Street." Plath took a step by establishing a relationship with this literary agent, who assisted her in sending out short stories to magazines. In Plath's address book, with the Sylvia Plath Collection at Smith, she has a listing for Jennifer Hassell at A.M. Heath and Co. Ltd., a literary agency at 35 Dover Street, London. Plath sent the stories she wrote that autumn to Hassell for consideration. It is possible to date uncollected stories such as "The

Lucky Stone," "A Winter's Tale," and "Shadow Girl" from this period. The tone of the stories, including the general voice of the protagonists, loosely resembles that of Esther Greenwood in *The Bell Jar*. "The Lucky Stone" is a story of a woman's rebellion and romance set in a Whitby bed and breakfast. "A Winter's Tale," is a romance set on the Yorkshire moors and shares its title with a poem Plath wrote and then published in *The New Yorker*. In "Shadow Girl," a young woman struggles to free herself and live individually from her father's success. While in Heptonstall, Plath made arrangements to meet with Hassell in January.

As 1961 approached, the Hughes's returned to London. Plath was troubled by repeated bouts of sinus infection. She also had pain from her appendix and sought advice from her doctor and family on whether she should have it removed. She was anxious to hear from her agent if the stories she submitted would be accepted, but there was no news to report. The BBC interviewed Plath and Hughes for their series about husbands and wives in the same profession called "Two of a Kind." The interview was broadcast several times in January and February, landing the Hughes's a nice fee. Impressed by the two poems she read the previous year, the BBC began to regularly seek Plath for their broadcasts.

Plath took a part-time job doing various editing tasks for a magazine called *The Bookseller*. By January 27, however, her appendix grew increasingly troublesome and the decision was made to have it taken out in February. Her primary concerns were Frieda and the recent discovery that she was pregnant again. She asked her mother, who was planning to visit in June and July, to reschedule her trip so she could be present for the baby's birth in mid-August. (*Letters Home*, 406) On February 1, Plath and Hughes met Theodore Roethke at a party; Plath had always wanted to meet him, "as I find he is my influence." (*Letters Home*, 407)

On Monday, February 6, Plath had a miscarriage. She was extremely sad at first, but then decided to plunge into work as a cure for her sorrow. She wrote a brilliant, sensitive poem about her experience on February 11. "Parliament Hill Fields" is about a walk Plath took on part of Hampstead Heath. The speaker walks alone, mourning the loss of an unborn child. She grows happier thinking of her daughter, safe and warm at home during winter. The poem begins,

> "On this bald hill the new year hones its edge.
> Faceless and pale as china
> The round sky goes on minding its business.
> Your absence is inconspicuous;
> Nobody can tell what I lack." (*Collected Poems*, 152)

Plath was now discovering her poetic voice, finally breaking free from influences such as Wallace Stevens, Yeats, and Roethke.

Throughout February, Plath produced a handful of good poems. She was commissioned to write a poem for a festival that summer. (*Letters Home*, 408) She was also asked to edit the booklet, *American Poetry Now* for the influential *Critical Quarterly*. With the subjects of children and childbirth still on her mind, she wrote "Face Lift," "Morning Song," which memorably begins "Love set you going like a fat gold watch," and "Barren Woman," within one week. (*Collected Poems*, 156) Her poems were growing increasingly personal, but her writing was also becoming more casual and recognizable. Toward the end of February, she was scheduled to have her appendix removed. She entered the hospital on February 26 and stayed until March 10. She was visited every evening by Hughes, who brought her food to make up for the hospital's food; his visits cheered her immensely. On February 28, he handed Plath a letter from *The New Yorker* with a check for $100 enclosed, paying her for "first reading" rights on all her new poems for one year. During her recovery she was required to stay in bed much of the time. She brought a notebook with her so she could write down observations, which proved very valuable. Making notes on different female patients in her ward, she wrote of hospital life in novelistic detail. Plath was released by March 10, under advice from her doctor to "behave like a lady" and rest. (*Letters Home*, 413)

In the spring, the Merwins returned to their house in France, again leaving their study available to Hughes and Plath. She wrote two hospital poems, "In Plaster" and "Tulips," on her first day in the study, March 18. Plath revisited her own leg break from 1953 in "In Plaster," mixed with details from her recent hospital stay. Although Plath continued to write poems that she felt exceeded previous efforts, "Tulips," accepted by *The New Yorker*, represented a breakthrough of a different kind. The poetry she began writing would be labeled "confessional" in the coming years. "Tulips" was her most openly "confessional" poem to date. The speaker of the poem, recovering in the hospital, is given a vase of red tulips. Their color was too loud and infringed upon the peaceful whiteness of her hospital room. In the end, she wished they would be removed because they reminded her that she was unhealthy. Plath's poems came easily now; she gained confidence in her writing and no longer needed much time to compose them. She also wrote, "I am Vertical" toward the end of March, the last poem she completed until "Insomniac" in May. "Insomniac" won a Guinness Poetry Award and was printed in the 1960/61 *Guinness Book of Poetry* and in the *Handbook of the Cheltenham Festival of Literature* in 1962.

In early May, Plath received good news: the publisher Alfred A. Knopf, in the United States, accepted *The Colossus*. To be safe, they requested Plath cut ten poems, several of which were a part of her "Poem for a Birthday" section at the end. They made the reduction because some of the poems, they felt, borrowed too freely from Roethke. Regardless of the cuts, with this success Plath felt happy and inspired to write. She took full advantage of the Merwins' study, writing in the morning seven days a week throughout the spring. She wrote some poems and a short story, "Day of Success," but spent most of her time drafting a novel. At the same time Knopf accepted *The Colossus*, Plath became pregnant for a third time, with the baby due in January 1962.

During the same period, Plath revisited a concept for a story she had developed a few years earlier. After a previous session with Dr. Beuscher, Plath had written the following in her journal: "There is an increasing market for mental-hospital stuff. I am a fool if I don't relive, recreate it." (*Journals*, 495) With this idea in mind, she set out to write a novel, which she planned to call *The*

*Bell Jar.* Her two major influences were *The Snake Pit* by Mary Jane Ward and *The Catcher in the Rye* by J.D. Salinger. Many of the stories Plath wrote in Boston and London helped her gear up for the longer project of writing a novel. In particular, one of Plath's greatest struggles in writing short fiction was finding the right voice. However, the writing came easier than she expected; she manipulated time and merged aspects of certain people she knew to create her characters. Some of the character names and traits developed in the short stories were to be interlaced with her personal history. The story vaguely disguised many of her experiences from 1953: a young woman's month-long internship as a Guest Editor at a woman's magazine in New York City, her subsequent depression, breakdown, and suicide attempt.

On her stolen Smith College memorandum paper, Plath made notes for twenty chapters. The notes are mostly based on real events, revealing names and places that are masked in the finished work. Because the idea to write a story or novel on the subject of her breakdown and recovery gestated for at least two years, the outline and writing came swiftly. By revisiting many emotional experiences from her past, especially after her traumatic miscarriage in February, Plath was released from a creative stranglehold she had had for years. She mentioned next to nothing of the novel to her mother; only making references to being very productive in the Merwins' study. (*Letters Home*, 416) In a letter to her college friend, Ann Davidow Goodman, dated April 27, she reports that she is one-third done with the novel. She confides her excitement about writing the novel and her intention to publish it under a pseudonym.[10] Plath completed a draft that spring, and finished it by August; Plath then sent it to James Michie at Heinemann. The final manuscript was very close to her outline, indicating her focus and skill throughout the process.

Plath chose the name "Esther Greenwood" for her protagonist. The important role of her boyfriend, Dick Norton, was the character named Buddy Willard. She called the doctor that performed ECT on her at his private hospital "Dr. Gordon," his name originating from her ex-boyfriend, Gordon Lameyer. Olive Higgins Prouty, the benefactress, responsible for her real life and fictional scholarship to college, and financial support during her treatment and recovery, was presented as "Philomena Guinea." A guinea was a form of British currency at the time, which perhaps inspired the name of Esther Greenwood's benefactress. There were very few family friends left out of Plath's novel. She knew the portrayals were unkind, but she felt compelled to merge and purge these experiences, which had been building up in her for nearly a decade.[11] Writing this novel was a brave act, although Plath eventually shrugged it off in a letter to Warren a year later, "I am a writer ... and have had my first novel accepted (this is a secret; it is a pot-boiler and no one must read it!)" (*Letters Home*, 472)

In the meantime, Plath's reputation as a poet was slowly growing in the London literary scene; in early June she made a recording for the BBC in their "Living Poet" series, both reading poems and giving commentary on them. Other poets in the series were such luminaries as Robert Lowell, Stanley Kunitz, and Roethke; Plath was honored to be among their company. Though she was now entrenched in England, Plath still considered herself an American poet and looked to other American poets for inspiration.

News of Plath's pregnancy coincided with her mother's visit. Aurelia arrived in mid-June to meet her granddaughter. She took care of Frieda starting on June 30, when Plath and Hughes left to cross the English Channel in their new car. They drove leisurely through France, seeing Berck-Plage on the Normandy coast, Finisterre, and the Dordogne. They stayed less than a week at the Merwins' farmhouse in Lacan de Loubressac, in south-central France, before returning to London on July 13. Their next adventure, after several days rest, was to Yorkshire, where after five years of marriage, the in-laws finally met. Aurelia was impressed by the Yorkshire landscape and became friends with Edith Hughes. Hughes thought about buying a house in Yorkshire, but Plath found the climate unwelcoming most of the time.[12] She was also unsure of how the Hughes family accepted her, or if they even liked her at all. Plath's only poem from July is "The Rival." Around this time, she also wrote "Stars Over the Dordogne." Aurelia was again a babysitter when her daughter and son-in-law traveled southwest of London to Devon to look at houses. They were interested in about eight when they left, easily narrowing the choice to one by their return.

They settled on a house called Court Green, located in North Tawton, a small Devonshire town. The house previously belonged to Sir and Lady Arundel. It had more than enough space for the family, but was in need of enough work to keep them busy for some time. Court Green, surrounded by a wall, had nine rooms plus an attic, stables, a disused tennis court, nearly three acres of land, and seventy apple trees. By all descriptions it was considered a manor house and its size gave the impression of being deep-set in the country. The house was in the town, adjacent to the church and cemetery. Although they had nearly enough to pay for the house outright, Plath and Hughes accepted a loan of £500 from each of their parents and took out a small bank loan to pay for the house. The Arundels would be gone by late August, giving the Hughes just enough time to pack and sublet their flat. Plath was very happy at the prospect of moving into Court Green: "I look forward to sampling our apples, making sauce, and anticipating our bank of spring daffodils. I think both of us will produce lots of work." (*Letters Home*, 422)

On August 4, Aurelia returned to the United States. On the whole, Plath found it very difficult to be around her mother; she preferred the safe distance of letter writing as the basis for their relationship. Writing *The Bell Jar* meant Plath had to contend with her inner demons, her mother being one of them, and the project subsequently increased Plath's stress. She signed the contract for Knopf's edition of *The Colossus* on August 16, hopeful of a publication date in the spring of 1962. During the wait for publication, Plath and Hughes had to focus on domestic issues.

Only halfway through their lease at Chalcot Square, the Hughes's set out to interview prospective sublet candidates. The Hughes's decided to impose a subletting fee to cover their expenses in modifying the flat. (*Letters Home*, 423) They began interviewing people in mid-August, and were surprised so many people responded to their ad. One potential candidate handed them a check immediately for the flat, but they decided to destroy it, as they much preferred a young couple, Assia and David Wevill.

David Wevill, born in Canada, was an aspiring poet and his wife, Assia, of German and Russian parentage and strikingly beautiful, worked for an advertising agency. The two couples got along nicely from the start. They had dinner shortly after they met, and the Hughes's gladly sublet their flat to them. The Wevills were immediately invited to visit them in North Tawton the following spring. The Wevills were not the only couple they had over for a farewell dinner; they also hosted the Macedos and the Sillitoes before the month was out. Plath had met the Portuguese poet, Helder Macedo, and his wife, Suzette, the previous spring.

As the Hughes packed up their flat to move to the country, *London Magazine* published six of Plath's poems in their August issue. She was four months pregnant and embarking on a major move, with major consequences.

# CHAPTER SEVEN

# The Triumphant Fulfillment

*And by the way, everything in life is writable about if you have the outgoing guts to do it, and the imagination to improvise. The worst enemy to creativity is self-doubt.*

—Sylvia Plath

APPROXIMATELY FOUR OR FIVE hours from London, North Tawton is twenty miles outside of Exeter. North Tawton was small and quiet, having little more than a post office, a green grocer's, a bank, and a car repair garage in the town's market square. The spire on St. Peter's Church, an Anglican Church, was visible from many viewpoints. Just west outside the town center, the River Taw flowed, flanked by fields, row houses, and a disused wool factory. In 1961 the population was under eleven hundred—a quiet community.[1] The view from Barton Hill, on the opposite side of town from the river was a lowland with Dartmoor's famous tors rising in the distance. A tor is a large mound of rocks that can be found on hilltops. In southwest England there are many tors, notably on Dartmoor and Bodmin Moor. The closest towns are Okehamton, Crediton, and Winkleigh. When the Hughes's moved into Court Green on August 31, much work needed to be done on the house. Their initial impression was positive and, as they became acquainted with the town and the townspeople, they grew more pleased with the move.

Throughout the fall of 1961, Plath was busy fixing up the house. The move into Court Green provided her with something she had not had since her days at Whitstead—a room of her own. Plath's study, on the second floor, was where she wrote every morning, on a large elm table Hughes and Warren had made for her. Plath always situated her desk to be by a window; the view she had was over their expansive front lawn, the large wall dividing her property from the church, the church itself, as well as a big Yew tree and a giant Wych Elm. While Plath loved Court Green for its spaciousness and peace, she also loved it because it provided an environment in which she could work alone; writing in the Merwins' study had shown her how much she could accomplish in solitude.

The first poems written at Court Green, "Wuthering Heights," "Blackberrying," and "Finisterre" are all remembrances of landscapes: West Yorkshire, the coast in Devon, and Brittany in France. Like "Stars Over the Dordogne," the language of the poems is factual and highly visual, with an underlying sense of excess and unease. As much as Plath loved living in the country, it was clearly more suited to Hughes' taste. They arranged to have Nancy Axworthy, a local, come to clean the house regularly, affording both more time to write.

Her next poem explored the human body, "The Surgeon at 2 A.M.," inspired by her stay at St. Pancras Hospital in March; after this she paused in her writing. Plath's concerns became centered on the domestic: baking, sewing on her new Singer machine, furnishing Court Green, and gardening. She had learned recently that her short story, "The Lucky Stone" had been sold to *My Weekly* and was encouraged by this to continue writing for women's magazines; equally encouraging was the news that her poem, "Insomniac" had won one of the £75 Guinness poetry prizes and that she was expected to go to Goldsmiths Hall in London for the ceremony later that month. The money would go directly toward their moving expenses, by far their biggest concern.

Plath was also determined to connect with the town and

decided to attend service at St. Peter's church next door. (*Letters Home*, 431) As a Unitarian she did not believe in the trinity, but enjoyed the sound of the bells and the visual and aural beauty of the service. She was rather disappointed in the sermon, thinking it was suited to smaller-minded people. Plath wanted a more convincing and charismatic style of preaching, like the one she had known at the Wellesley Unitarian church.

Much earlier in that morning of October 21, Plath had written a poem about the view of the church from outside Court Green. "The Moon and the Yew Tree," a poem suggested by Hughes after they had watched the full moon above the yew tree the previous sleepless night, was a revelation. In this poem, Plath finds her voice, called the *Ariel* voice, though it had been evident since she had written "Tulips" in March. "The Moon and the Yew Tree" was Plath's latest poem on inner and outer landscape, and the overall meaning of it depressed Hughes.[2]

By the end of October, Plath wrote her final poems of 1961: "Last Words," "Mirror," and "The Babysitters." "Mirror," one of Plath's most studied poems today, challenges its readers. The speaker adopts the mannerisms of a mirror, becoming "not cruel, only truthful." (*Collected Poems*, 173) Plath's poetry did indeed take a decided turn to the more "truthful." The last poem Plath wrote in 1961, "The Babysitters," recalls her summer in Swampscott. The poem was influenced by the work of Lowell and Sexton, emoting fondness and sadness, but not nostalgia. Plath was doing other writing besides poems and short stories in October. She joined Hughes in writing book reviews for the *New Statesman*, choosing children's literature first, and rejoicing in the nearly fifty free books they had for Frieda. (*Letters Home*, 433) North Tawton had no bookshop, and the closest library was in Exeter, roughly an hour drive away.

In late October, Plath went to London by herself to accept her Guinness prize and read at the ceremony alongside other poets, including Richard Murphy and Robert Graves, author of *The White Goddess*.[3] She also took time to meet with an agent to inquire about selling her poetry manuscripts, and had a meeting with an editor at a women's magazine. She stayed with novelist

Alan Sillitoe and his wife, Ruth Fainlight. Between settling in North Tawton and professional engagements, Plath was very busy throughout the autumn. Winter was approaching, months Plath expected to be dour. (*Letters Home*, 435)

In November, Plath was overjoyed to find out that she had won a Saxton grant worth $2000; she had to give the committee quarterly reports on a work of fiction and was relieved to have *The Bell Jar* already done. The Saxton grant marked Plath's first major financial contribution to the marriage in nearly three years, since she left her teaching position at Smith. The first installment came that month, and Plath also made money by selling her poetry manuscripts from *The Colossus* to Indiana University, just as Hughes had. *The New Yorker* accepted "Blackberrying." Plath even received a fan letter from another writer for her story in *My Weekly*.[4] She was also asked by the *Critical Quarterly* to edit an anthology of American poets. When *American Poetry Now* was issued early the next year it sold well. With these successes, Plath could, for once, rest as she prepared Court Green for winter and the arrival of her second baby.

After reading an article in *The Nation* called "Juggernaut, the Warfare State," Plath sunk into a mild depression. The article reassured her that relocating to England from America was the proper decision, though she felt much concern for Frieda and the new baby. (*Letters Home*, 437–38) The Cold War was becoming tenser, and Plath, now a housewife and mother, had more concern than ever about a possible nuclear war between the United States and Russia. Once over this depression, she reverted to being blissful and interested again in domestic chores. (*Letters Home*, 439) She made curtains out of red corduroy for the living room and waited for the baby, due on January 11.

Plath went into labor on the evening of January 17. Together she, Nurse Winifred Davies, and Hughes waited. Nurse Davies had only one cylinder of gas for Plath to use and the gas ran out before Plath was ready. After great pain, Nicholas Farrar Hughes was born just before midnight. As she wrote, "this great bluish, glistening boy shot out onto the bed ... howling lustily." (*Letters Home*, 443) Nicholas had quite a different temperament compared to Frieda; everything about him was Hughes-like. (*Letters Home*, 444) As Plath grew comfortable with Nicholas, she looked forward to writing again.

*London Magazine* published "In Plaster" in their February issue. They also published a small essay by Plath in which she reflected upon the larger world; the magazine called it "Context." Of her poems, Plath wrote, "They are not about the terrors of mass extinction, but about the bleakness of the moon over a yew tree ... In a sense, these poems are deflections." (*Johnny Panic*, 64) Plath's response, written several months earlier, could stand as her view of poetry for most of her writing life; though clearly aware of politics, she had yet to figure out how to use the outside world in her writing.

In March, Plath was commissioned by the BBC to write a radio play. Inspired by both Ingmar Bergman's film, *Brink of Life*, and Dylan Thomas's verse play *Under Milk Wood*, Plath wrote a long verse poem for three voices on pregnancy and childbirth. The voices of "Three Women" include a happy mother, a young woman who has a miscarriage, and a student who gives her baby up for adoption. Also that month Plath had five poems appear in *Poetry* (Chicago), including "Stars Over the Dordogne" and "Love Letter."

Slowly, the Hughes's were making acquaintances in North Tawton. Plath obligatorily hosted and attended tea with some of these Devonians. She spent a decent amount of time with the Tyrer family; George, the bank manager, his wife, Marjorie, and their teenage daughter, Nicola, who bothered her. Hughes was now famous enough that the Tyrers sent Nicola to Court Green often; she was young and charming, and this stirred Plath's jealousy.[5] By late March, Plath felt more at home in North Tawton than she would again. On March 25, Frieda and Nicholas were baptized at St. Peter's, though she no longer attended services there due to the sermons. Plath's study, which was being furnished bit by bit, acted as her own church. (*Letters Home*, 450)

After hearing a program on Laura Riding's poetry in early April, she wrote "Little Fugue," a poem about her father.[6] Within a week, Plath had written several more poems, including "Among the Narcissi," "Crossing the Water," "An Appearance," and "Pheasant." The general tone of these poems is cool and observant; death and life are held in balance. The most complex of the April poems, however, is "Little Fugue," in which Plath looks at her own faulty connection with her father, deconstructing him from his colossal stature; he now has "one leg, and a Prussian mind."

Later in April, Marvin Kane interviewed Plath for the BBC, and *The New Yorker* published "Tulips." Plath was also busy domestically, picking and selling hundreds of daffodils, painting furniture, and waiting for spring to arrive. Even though the winter was long, she had much to look forward to, including the United States publication of *The Colossus* in May and Aurelia's visit that summer.

Her last poem in April was "Elm." Unlike her other poems, "Elm," about the large Wych Elm she could see from her study, is dominated by fear. "Elm" also has an element of ecological panic. The atmosphere the poem gives is dark; the elm is poisonous and troubling. When it was eventually published, it was titled "The Elm Speaks" to facilitate understanding the speaker from its listener.[7] Plath looked to the elm for advice; the elm answers unspoken questions. Both Plath and the elm are "inhabited" by something dangerous. The ancient elm confesses to being "incapable of more knowledge," ultimately telling Plath that what has been troubling her, "are the isolate, slow faults/ That kill, that kill, that kill." (*Collected Poems*, 193) One answer in "Elm" to Plath's unspoken question is: "Love is a shadow." (*Collected Poems*, 192) From this line it can be inferred there was dissonance in her life.

Though the Tyrers were still around, the main neighbors they dealt with were Rose and Percy Key, who lived in one of the cottages lining their drive. Rose often called on Hughes to help move Percy, who was dying, from room to room. Percy suffered a stroke in mid-April, and Plath may have seen his deterioration as a double to her father.

Hughes's Aunt Hilda and cousin Vicky came down to stay over Easter weekend, helping around the house and getting to know Nicholas. Court Green's daffodils, primroses, hyacinths, and apple and cherry trees, were all in bloom, which lifted Plath's spirits immeasurably. (*Letters Home*, 454) In early May, the novelist, Alan Sillitoe and his poet-wife, Ruth Fainlight, visited with their own newborn, David. Plath read some of her recent poems to Fainlight and was so pleased at her reaction to "Elm" that she dedicated it to her. Assia and David Wevill, who were subletting Chalcot Square, arrived for a weekend stay at Court Green later in the month. The four listened to a record of Robert Lowell reading his poems, and Plath learned more about Assia's background, including her two previous marriages and impressive worldly experiences.

What must have interested Plath the most was Assia's childhood; when she was a young girl, her half-Jewish family escaped from Nazi Germany to Palestine, and then to Canada. Assia knew several languages and wanted to work as a poet and translator. Initially, Plath liked the Wevills; they were a break from her country life. At some point, Plath realized that sensual energy was flowing between Hughes and Assia; as a result, she became fearful and suspicious. Assia was elegant and well-dressed, as opposed to Plath, who at this time was much more homely and mothering two small children. If Plath saw Assia as competition, she knew that Assia was a real rival.

On May 21, the morning after the Wevills left, Plath wrote; after a slow start, she produced "The Rabbit Catcher" and "Event," two personal poems on the troubled state of her marriage. "The Rabbit Catcher" is a view of male-female relations in general, and her own voiceless stance in her marriage. Hughes was dismayed by "Event"; he did not believe in writing poetry about his personal life. Plath sent "Event" to Alvarez at the *Observer*, nevertheless.

Knopf published *The Colossus* in the United States. It was barely reviewed that spring, not even in New York or Boston.[8] It could be that Plath's work was no longer fashionable, but the poems in *The Colossus* were over two years old. Plath's voice had developed deeply since 1960; and she was progressing evenly with 'confessional' poets like Lowell and Sexton. Plath may have been dismayed at the lack of critical attention, but professionally she continued to progress; in early June, the BBC accepted "Three

Women." The *New Statesman* printed two book reviews by Plath, including one of a biography of Napoleon's wife, Josephine.

In late May, Plath wrote "Apprehensions," before the arrival of Hughes's parents and his Uncle Walt. In these May poems, Plath silently questions her marriage, though by all appearances the marriage was steady. Alvarez visited on June 8, and Plath showed him Court Green, telling him she would like for him to see her new poems. (Alvarez, *Savage God*, 28)

Throughout June, Plath worked in the garden; she also readied the house for Aurelia's stay. On June 7, Plath and Hughes attended a meeting of the Devon Beekeepers, headed by a man called Charlie Pollard. They met at Pollard's house in Mill Lane, on the River Taw, near the old wool factory. At the meeting, the Hughes's met other locals interested in beekeeping and they were able to obtain a free hive. This was a welcome event—meeting new, local people—in the wake of their spring visitors from London. She also met David and Elizabeth Compton, who lived out in the country north of Court Green.[9]

Despite these new friendships, Plath missed London, especially the cultural scene. In late June, Aurelia arrived at Court Green, seeing for the first time the house she helped purchase. Percy Key died on June 29; after the funeral, Plath wrote a long poem, which she called "Berck-Plage." The previous summer Plath and Hughes visited Berck-Plage, along the Normandy coast, on their way to visit the Merwins. In its seven parts, "Berck-Plage" intertwines the invalids at a military hospital there with Percy Key's death and funeral. In addition, Hughes and Assia Wevill had begun having an affair. He traveled to and from London for various reasons, but when confronted by Plath, Hughes denied everything. (Feinstein, 126) Not persuaded, Plath wrote "The Other" on July 2, presenting her suspicions in writing.

On July 9, upon returning to Court Green from a day trip with her mother to Exeter, Plath answered a phone call intended for Hughes. Assia tried to disguise her voice, but Plath knew it was her. She gave the phone to Hughes; after he hung up, she ripped the phone from the wall. She left Court Green with Frieda and Nicholas and went to the Comptons'. Elizabeth remembered that upon Plath's arrival she was crying and saying her milk had gone dry, but even worse, Hughes was having an affair. (Feinstein, 127) Plath stayed with the Comptons that night, ashamed that her mother witnessed the discovery of the affair. Aurelia moved in with Winifred Davies for the rest of her stay, visiting Court Green and spending most of her time with the children. Plath wrote "Words heard, by accident, over the phone" in her rage; she then wrote "Poppies in July," a poem in which the speaker longs for escape, by fire or the oblivion of opiates.

The next day, she sent Alvarez "The Rabbit Catcher," "Event," and "Elm," since she knew that he understood what she was doing poetically. With her doubts about Hughes coming true, Plath turned to Alvarez for trust with her writing. Though the *Observer* only bought "Event," they also published "The Rival," "Finisterre," and "Crossing the Water" in 1962; *Harper's Magazine* published "Private Ground." Plath and Hughes traveled to Bangor, Wales for a special evening of readings hosted by *Critical Quarterly*, keeping up appearances that their relationship was well.

On August 4, Aurelia departed from Court Green. She knew upon leaving that Plath and Hughes were going to try to live apart. In line with her beekeeping, Plath wrote a fragment of a poem that is now titled, "Stings (2)." Her inspiration failed her and the poem was set aside. One evening she gathered all of Hughess' papers on his desk, including letters, and made a bonfire, and wrote "Burning the Letters." This is a poem not just about vengeance but also poetic immortality; it was drafted, in part, on the verso of a copy of Hughes's "The Thought-Fox." In "Burning the Letters" Plath also mentions a fox, so in an ironic way, Hughes was still inspiring her work, though he had not given her any new subject lists. Plath and Hughes went to London in mid-August, as Olive Higgins Prouty was visiting and wanted to see them. They saw the Agatha Christie play, *The Mousetrap* and were put up at Prouty's hotel, The Connaught. They also dined with her, and the two were able to put aside their differences to enjoy the meal. Prouty, long Plath's mentor, still meant a great deal to her and was invited to visit Court Green.

Plath was soon ill and feverish, losing weight, and unable to write. She relied on the Comptons and Winifred Davies for comfort and support. "Three Women" was broadcast on the BBC on August 19. She saw Hughes, who was living with various friends in London, on the weekend. Plath wanted the trial separation to be final. On August 27, she wrote to her mother with details of their trial separation, explaining that her writing had suffered as much as her life, and recently her health had started to suffer, too. (*Letters Home*, 460)

Plath wanted to take some time away from Court Green, so she wrote to Richard Murphy, a poet she knew who lived in Cleggan, Ireland, near Galway. Murphy was named the winner of the 1962 Guinness Poetry Prize. Plath, who won the award the previous year, wrote to him with congratulations. She asked if he could accommodate herself and Hughes at his home. Plath and Hughes arrived in Dublin on September 11, staying the night with Jack and Marie Sweeney, old Boston acquaintances. They arrived at Murphy's cottage the next day; it was Plath's first visit to Ireland. She hoped to find a place to rent for the winter, preferably on the sea, to cope with the disintegration of her marriage. (*Letters Home*, 461) Initially, the stay at Murphy's cottage went well as Plath found a cottage to rent nearby. The three visited Coole Park, where they climbed Yeats' Tower; Plath made a wish as she threw coins down into the stream. They also went sailing one day, and Murphy recalls that Plath was immensely happy. (Stevenson, 349)

Hughes abruptly left Murphy's cottage on September 15. The night before all had seemed well, with the Irish poet, Thomas Kinsella arriving that day to visit Murphy. The four had dined and talked pleasantly, but now Hughes was missing. This embarrassed Plath, who had thought of this trip as an attempt at reconciling her relationship with Hughes. She told Murphy that Hughes went to visit a painter in another county and then to do some salmon fishing; but, in reality, she did not know where he had gone.[10] Murphy asked Plath to leave because Cleggan was a small village and he was nervous of the potential rumors if Plath stayed on at his cottage. She returned to Dublin with Kinsella and then returned to Court Green the next day.

When Plath arrived at Court Green, a vague note from Hughes sent from London was waiting for her. Dr. Buescher, whom she had written to for advice on how to deal with Hughes's behavior, encouraged Plath to get a divorce and to do so immediately, while the evidence was still apparent. By September 24, Plath had contacted her accountant, who in turn recommended a lawyer. Plath was certain her decision to obtain a legal separation from Hughes was the correct action to take. If the separation were made legal, Plath hoped she could avoid going to court by getting Hughes to give her an allowance. This decisive action, as painful as it was, gave Plath some sense of control. She was now taking sleeping pills for her recently developed insomnia.

The effect of the sleeping pills Plath was taking wore off around four in the morning. The children generally did not need her until around eight, so Plath began writing poems again, taking advantage of this quiet. On September 26, Plath wrote "For a Fatherless Son," a poem addressed to Nicholas about her joy in his not knowing that his father was away. She wrote to Prouty that Hughes was now becoming a stranger. Hughes had come by that day to Court Green, but Plath turned him away, informing him that she wanted a separation and to come back later for his belongings. On September 30, she wrote "A Birthday Present," a poem in which death "stands at my window, big as the sky." (*Collected Poems,* 207)

The sporadic writing Plath had been doing for the better part of the year was like a crack in a dam. In October 1962, the crack fissured, the dam broke, and Sylvia Plath became a poet of mythic stature. Drafting poems almost exclusively on her pilfered, pink Smith College memorandum paper, Plath wrote on paper already used, mostly on the verses of pages from drafts of *The Bell Jar.* In the twenty-five October poems, Plath composed poetry with a newfound control and confidence over her subject and language. The solid, uninterrupted time in her study each morning aided her in this accomplishment; her productivity has been compared only to John Keats, who in 1818 wrote the majority of his famous poems. Despite the number of poems she wrote, they did not arrive spontaneously. They were carefully crafted poems, sharp and feminine; she spoke them as she wrote, as if by dictation. (Orr, 170)

On October 1, Plath wrote "The Detective," and the next day "The Courage of Shutting-Up." Both poems exploit her disintegrating marriage, and her own silence and loss of presence. From October 3 to 7, Plath wrote five poems about bees: "The Bee Meeting," "The Arrival of the Bee Box," "Stings" "The Swarm," and "Wintering." For "The Bee Meeting" and "The Arrival of the Bee Box," Plath took the new beekeeping experiences from her June 1962 journals. As an outsider in the town's bee society, she was scared but refused to leave, ultimately gaining acceptance and control over her hive. "Stings" is a poem of self-discovery in which Plath compares herself to the respected queen bee. "The Swarm" is an antiwar poem, using Napoleon as an example of military hubris. "Wintering" closes the sequence with rebirth and the promise of "spring."

For the first time since her early poetry, Plath was writing about history and politics, making her poems more open to the outside world. She had continued to see the Comptons and other sympathetic people, either at their homes or at Court Green. Hughes returned on October 4, he collected his belongings and agreed to give her a £1000 a year allowance for utilities and childcare; Plath wanted no money for herself. She wrote "A Secret" on October 10; the next day, she wrote "The Applicant," a very humorous poem about the commercial and dehumanizing aspects of marriage. Hughes moved out of Court Green that day, and Plath wrote to her mother that she was pleased with the writing she had been doing of late. (*Letters Home*, 466) With Hughes gone, Plath wrote "Daddy," a complex look at herself, her father, and Hughes; the poem was written in a deceptively light style, but passionate and uncompromising all the same.

After a weekend in Cornwall, Plath continued on October 16 with "Medusa," a vicious poem about her relationship with her mother. That same day she told her mother, "I am a genius of a writer; I have it in me. I am writing the best poems of my life; they will make my name." (*Letters Home*, 468) Plath developed another fever at this time; Aurelia had been trying to convince Plath to return to Wellesley, but Plath refused, even for the holidays. From October 17 to 19, Plath wrote "The Jailer," "Lesbos," and "Stopped Dead." In "The Jailer," Plath is a fevered, tortured captive, who is brutalized and has died numerous times: "Hung, starved, burned, hooked." (*Collected Poems,* 227) By this time, she had also learned that Heinemann had accepted *The Bell Jar* and scheduled to publish it in January 1963.

Plath wrote "Fever 103°," a poem on purity, sin, and sexual renewal on October 20 and the next day, "Amnesiac" and "Lyonnesse," poems of historical and personal forgetfulness. On October 24, she wrote "Cut" and dedicated it to her young, live-in nanny, Susan O'Neill-Roe.[11] Susan gave Plath some relief and enabled her to write at night as well as early in the morning. She continued on her blaze, writing a satirical poem, "The Tour" and a tender poem, "By Candlelight." Between October 23 and 29, Plath wrote one of her most famous poems, "Lady Lazarus"; this poem of female subjugation and defiance, death and rebirth, has some of her most famous lines. She also wrote "Poppies in October," "Nick and the Candlestick," and "Purdah" before the end of the month; on her birthday she wrote "Ariel."

On October 27, Plath turned thirty. She went out in the morning, as she did every Saturday, to take riding lessons at a local stable on Dartmoor. "Ariel" is a poem of incredible speed and dexterity and named after the horse she rode. Even though Plath had been writing brilliant poems all month, "Ariel" was the penultimate; it is a poem about *her* rebirth, about freedom and release.[12] Plath traveled to London on October 29 to record her poems at the BBC. She met with Alvarez to read her new poems. The next day, she ate lunch with Peter Orr from the BBC, then read many of her new poems, and concluded with a short interview. Orr asked her where her poems came from—books or her life—and her response was, "I think that personal experience is very important, but certainly it shouldn't be a kind of shut-box and mirror-looking, narcissistic experience." (Orr, 169–70)

Upon returning to Court Green, Plath ruled out wintering in Ireland and decided to move back to London. She hoped Hughes would be more responsible about the children if he could visit them on a regular basis. She wanted to enter Frieda into a neighborhood day school and have a nanny as well. On November 4, she returned to London to look for a flat, with Hughes's help. Her instincts brought her back to Primrose Hill, where Frieda was born. Surprised, she found a "To Let" sign for the top two floors of an unfurnished flat at 23 Fitzroy Road, in the house where Yeats had lived. Beside the front door, a blue plaque announced that Yeats had lived there for a time, and at the end of the block, a small green swatch of Primrose Hill was visible. She applied with Hughes to make the process easier; a single mother applying would not have been as likely to get the flat.

In early November, Plath wrote "The Couriers," "Getting There," "The Night Dances," and "Gulliver." Alternately mysterious and tender, these poems read as though they were from a different inspiration. Only "Getting There" has the emphatic energy of the October poems. "The Night Dances" poses her child's life against the cold vastness of the universe. Plath wrote "Thalidomide," "Letter in November," and "Death & Co." before she finally assembled her manuscript. She debated over the title of this collection, choosing at one point among *A Birthday Present*, *The Rabbit Catcher*, or *Daddy*. She finally settled on *Ariel*, the poem written on her thirtieth birthday.[13] There is no evidence suggesting Plath sent this manuscript to publishers. Plath's list of submitted poems, held now at Smith College, shows that she started sending these poems out on October 10, 1962. Over the next six weeks, she sent out batches of poems, on average, every four or five days. The many rejections she received possibly dissuaded her from sending the manuscript out, remembering the difficulty and disappointment of rejections she had with initial versions of *The Colossus*.

On November 16, she wrote "Years," a poem that contrasts life on earth with the static, eternal life of God and "The Fearful," a colder revisit of the fateful phone call in July. Plath's poetry seemed to change suddenly as she anticipated moving back to London. Though still fluent and definitely in her voice, she was now writing about larger subjects, such as religion and history, as illustrated in "Mary's Song."[14]

Professionally, Plath was busy—sending poems out as usual, answering letters in response to the broadcast of "Three Women," and having her long poem, "Berck-Plage" also broadcast on the BBC. At one point, she opened a collection of Yeats' plays for a message and received the following: "Get wine and food to give you strength and courage, and I will get the house ready."[15] (*Letters Homes*, 480) Although still uncertain over the Fitzroy Road flat, she welcomed any good omens. She was anxious to leave Court Green because some of the locals thought she and Hughes were perhaps never married, since so much mail came for "Miss Plath."

Despite financial help from her Aunt Dorothy, her mother, and Prouty, Plath wanted to be self-sufficient through her writing. *The New Yorker, London Magazine,* and *The Atlantic Monthly* were responsive, but between them only bought five poems. *The New Yorker*'s Howard Moss asked if he could only print part of "Amnesiac," leaving out the section later called "Lyonnesse." He also bought "Elm," but changed the title to "The Elm Speaks." Plath was always willing to have small changes made to her poems, as long as they would be published. Karl Miller of *The New Statesman* rejected the *Ariel* poems he received altogether. Instead, he gave Plath some more books to review, including one on Lord Byron's wife, which she was eager to read; by reviewing books, she could at least keep her name in print.

It is impossible to judge how disheartening these rejections were. Certainly she was baffled, as Alvarez liked her work, and she herself knew they were the best poems she had ever written. In the meantime, Heinemann had sent *The Bell Jar* to Knopf, Plath's American publisher.[16] Heinemann sent Plath the proofs to look over in November. The BBC continued to support her; the Home Services asked her to write a two-thousand-word piece on her childhood, which she titled "Ocean 1212-W" after her grandparents phone number. A complex and haunting essay, it evokes the ocean and her intense bond with it—a connection that she had been separated from in England. Recalling her childhood, a stage she claimed to be happiest in, the essay ends with the death of her father, which was equated with the loss of the sea. (*Johnny Panic,* 26)

Plath had been writing to Clarissa Roche, who was now living with her family in Kent, to come and visit her. Roche, who was busy with a newborn of her own, visited Court Green in November. During Roche's weekend stay, she heard about how terrible Hughes had been. Her anger with Hughes was mixed with sadness, Roche remembered. (Butscher, ed. 89) Roche could see that Plath had been writing as sheets of paper were scattered on her study floor; all that Plath needed was some help at home. Plath asked if she could visit her once she had moved in to her new flat. By now Plath was desperate to move and had given her mother's name, *Professor* A.S. Plath, as a guarantee, as well as paying a year's rent in advance. Throughout the fall, Plath had been working on a new novel, which she planned to call *Double Exposure*, but the circumstances were so hectic that she did not have a stretch of time to focus on it, as she had with *The Bell Jar*.

By November 29, Plath settled on the flat and was beside herself with joy. (*Letters Home*, 482) She was also continuing to sever herself from Hughes: "My solicitor is gathering the evidence necessary for a Divorce Petition. I think there should be no trouble as Ted is very cooperative." (*Letters Home*, 483) Buoyed by a large check from Aunt Dorothy, she set out to pack up her things, reap her apples and garden, and cut holly before her move. She was still writing, though at a slower pace. She wrote "Winter Trees" in late November, with trees once again representing women, with the speaker as an observer, distant and beautiful. She then wrote "Brasilia" and "Childless Woman" both harsher, with frigidity and violence from the outside world, and the vanity of the woman with no children again described.

Plath was now a single mother with two children, like her mother, and had to be their sole protector and help. Plath's exhilaration, seen in the *Ariel* poems, was now gone. Her more recent poetry, celebratory of the self, was replaced by her old stoicism. On December 3, Plath signed the lease for her new flat and arranged for the electricity to be turned on and the gas stove she had bought to be installed; she then returned to Court Green to pack.

Plath set off for London with Frieda and Nicholas on December 10, after relinquishing her bees. She had a local mover take what she could not fit in her Morris Traveler station wagon, leaving most of her furniture behind.[17] After having some trouble moving in (the electricity and gas still had to be connected, so she moved in by candlelight), she managed to have the stove and lights on by the end of the day. Plath was very happy to be back in her old neighborhood and pleased to be remembered. (Plath, *Letters Home*, 486) Plath was once again taking sleeping pills and eager to find a new live-in nanny. She preferred to have Susan O'Neill-Roe, but she was about to start work at a nearby London hospital for children. Plath loved working at home, "because then I don't miss any of the babies' antics. I adore them." (*Letters Home*, 488) However, she needed a nanny to help her so she could focus on her writing.

Alvarez had recently accepted "Ariel." His superiors, worried about the readers' response, changed the title to "The Horse." She had been asked by Douglas Cleverdon at the BBC to put together a list of her new poems for a future program and was asked permission from a radio station in Oslo, Norway to have a translation of "Three Women" for a radio broadcast. In the meantime, Plath was busy painting and furnishing her new flat to suit her tastes. (*Letters Home*, 491) She had also, with Prouty's help, bought more clothing. Plath was asked to judge the Cheltenham poetry contest again, and was readying herself for London social life, including the launch of *The Bell Jar* in January.

On December 16, "Event," the poem Hughes disliked, was published in the *Observer*. On the surface, her life was very much her own, but underneath, Plath was not as happy as her letters may have indicated. She had no phone and found life difficult without it; she had to use a public booth down the block to arrange meetings. One of the people she was now seeing again was Hughes, who would come regularly and often take Frieda and Nicholas to the zoo. It is hard to imagine what Plath felt upon seeing him again; she needed to see him because of their children. But some of Plath's friends, including her mother, felt that she missed Hughes and was still hoping for reconciliation with him, despite her earlier actions. For now Plath continued to live independently, though seeing Hughes again may have caused her to start seriously reconsidering what she wanted as she missed what they once had together. The days grew shorter, winter closed in, and Plath needed the company of others.

On Christmas Eve, Alvarez stopped by her flat on his way to a party. Plath wanted to begin a relationship with him, but Alvarez, a recent divorcee, had to turn Plath down. He described her that night as "different ... like a priestess emptied out by the rites of her cult ... I had never seen her so strained." (*Savage God*, 45–6) He heard several of her latest poems, and before he left, Plath broke down crying, pleading with him to stay. He left, and remembered knowing that he had let her down in an ultimate manner. (*Savage God*, 48) Hughes had spent Christmas in Yorkshire; he had invited Plath to join him, but she declined. Plath had Christmas dinner with the Macedos, who gave Frieda and Nicholas presents. The children also got clothes from Warren and Margaret, and Plath continued receiving money from Aurelia and Prouty to help with her continued expenses. Despite the various channels of support, Plath was slipping into a depression. She received a rejection she had not expected from Knopf, turning down *The Bell Jar*. Previously, any rejection she received could be endured with Hughes. Her creative work was severely hindered due to this rejection, and the mounting needs of the children and work to be done on her flat. On December 31, she managed to finish "Eavesdropper," a poem she started in October.

In January 1963, the harsh reality of winter set in. There had been some snow before Christmas, but in Devon there were twenty-foot drifts, and food and drink had to be brought in by helicopter. Plath, accustomed to snowy winters in Massachusetts, was initially delighted as it was her first *real* experience of winter in England. The deluge of snow came as a surprise to England; the country had very few snow removal vehicles. Plath was careful about going out since the streets were slick, and she had to be mindful of her children. (*Letters Home*, 494) Plath had gone to see Dr. Horder about her health; he gave her a tonic to help her gain weight, as she had lost a significant amount throughout the summer and fall. He also performed a chest x-ray, after he heard about her high fevers. But she again suffered from the flu and was too weak to do much; Hughes coming by weekly enabled her to rest. The children also had illnesses that winter, and she still had no phone.

Snow and ice continued to accumulate in what turned out to be the worst, coldest winter in England for over a century; there were frequent power outages and water pipes froze and burst. Plath tried her best, even under these conditions, to continue her life as a poet and freelance writer. On January 10, she went to the BBC to review a book of contemporary American poetry on the air. Then on January 13, "Winter Trees" appeared in the *Observer*, and the next day, she went to Heinemann's launch party for *The Bell Jar*. Published under a pseudonym, it was dedicated "to Elizabeth and David," the Comptons in Devon. The party was not as big and festive as Plath would have liked, though the Macedos did invite Doris Lessing, a writer Plath admired; Hughes was there as well. Plath, still trying to keep the novel a secret from her mother, did not write home about the party, but she did share news of a commission from *Punch* to write an article about American education, which she called "America! America!" Normally an upbeat letter writer, Plath did tell her mother about her exhaustion: "I just haven't felt to have any *identity* under the steamroller of decisions and responsibilities of this last half year, with the babies a constant demand ... How I would *like* to be self-supporting on my writing! But I need *time*. I guess I just need somebody to cheer me up by saying I've done all right so far." (*Letters Home*, 495–6)

Clarissa Roche stopped by Fitzroy Road for her visit. She found Plath's flat very neat and tidy, and Plath had a schedule of menus and the ingredients arranged in her kitchen. But Plath was too distracted to cook, so Roche made her dinner. They talked about the literary world and Plath's plans to write: "She told me she had the right sort of sick humor to turn out stories for *The New Yorker*. That would pay well. She could discipline herself, she said, to produce them quickly and leave plenty of time for poetry." (Butscher, ed., 92) Plath later greeted Paul Roche and the rest of their children as cheerful as ever; she described Plath as being a master of disguise. (Butscher, ed., 93) A few days later, Patty Goodall, a friend of Mildred Norton, dropped by Plath's to visit, and this disguising was in full effect. In a letter Goodall sent to Aurelia after her visit, she recalled that despite the bitter cold winter day, Plath's enthusiasm for having a visitor and conversation made it warm and inviting. (*Letters Home*, 496) She also told Aurelia that Plath "NEVER STOPPED TALKING," and that she was "interesting, fun, and full of charm." (*Letters Home*, 497)

Through the Macedos, Plath met a new couple with children, Gerry and Jillian Becker, who lived nearby off Barnsbury Square. She and the Beckers became friends, and in the coming weeks she would become closer to them. The writing Plath did from mid to late January should be considered among her best. She wrote "Snow Blitz" for *Punch*, about the recent terrible weather, with an American look at the situation in London. "Snow Blitz" is full of wonderful humor and, in the absence of journals for this period, is full of helpful personal details. She also completed her article, "America, America!"

Plath had been able to do this writing because she had found a nanny; by late January, she was also starting to write poetry again. Though they are as strong and beautiful as any of the *Ariel* poems, the last dozen poems that Plath wrote were markedly reserved and somber in tone and clearly suited for inclusion in another collection. On January 28, she wrote "The Munich Mannequins," "Totem," and "Child," as well as editing "Sheep in Fog," a poem first drafted in December. "The Munich Mannequins" recalls her time in Munich with Lameyer, the coldness and silence somehow dehumanizing. "Totem" is a grim, imagistic look at death, while "Child" is a tender poem addressed to her children, beginning, "Your clear eye is the one absolutely beautiful thing," and again celebrates their innocence. (*Collected Poems*, 265) "Sheep in Fog," is one of her greatest poems. It has symbols familiar from her *Ariel* poems, the horse in particular, but presented in a more sedate way.

On January 29, she wrote "Paralytic" and "Gigolo"; the first is about a man cut off from the world, seemingly content to be unable to move, and the second is a description of a vain and womanizing man. On February 1, she wrote two more poems,

"Kindness" and "Mystic." "Kindness" is about a woman, who claims sugar is a cure-all; but, the last lines, "The blood jet is poetry,/ There is no stopping it./ You hand me two children, two roses," show that kindness is good, perhaps necessary to artistic creation, and that writing goes on with or without her. "Mystic" is a poem about a need for a way to cope with intense experience, possibly a mystical one, that resolves itself with the rising sun and a sense of life in everything. The question Plath poses, "Is there no great love, only tenderness?" (*Collected Poems,* 269), indicates a longing that is never fulfilled.

Plath sent the following poems to *The New Yorker:* "Kindness," "Mystic," "Words," "Edge," "Balloons," and "Contusion."[18] "Words" is a poem about language and fate. It is in some ways emblematic of Plath's experience with writer's block and having her new work find sympathetic editors and publishers. The words themselves echo, travel, and return, no longer hers; this seems to be the way of things, as "fixed stars/ Govern a life." (*Collected Poems,* 270) The determination of the *Ariel* poems had given way to a kind of fatalism, but her voice was as strong as ever. She also completed "Edge," a beautiful, sensuous poem, about a woman who has died along with her two children; it is slightly mocking, but the black humor is subtle enough to be missed. The moon, largely absent from her recent poetry, observes coolly from her distance. Similarly, in "Contusion," there is an implied death, "The heart shuts,/ The sea slides back,/ The mirrors are sheeted." (*Collected Poems,* 271) "Balloons," possibly Plath's last poem, is completely different. In a happy, domestic scene, Frieda and Nicholas play with some animal-shaped balloons; it is a poem full of life, color, and wonder—of peace of a different kind.

Plath wrote letters to her college friend, Marcia Brown, and her mother in early February. The doubtfulness and discouragement she felt were plain; the letters she had been writing recently were very honest. After being implored to return to the United States, she once again declares that she has no intention of going back home. She had been seeing Hughes quite regularly because she wanted him to accept more liability for his children. (*Letters Home,* 498) The letters were not completely downtrodden; Plath reported that she had a chance to be on a BBC panel show, *The Critics*, that spring. Dr. Horder had recently put her on a course of antidepressants, and she took these in addition to her sleeping pills.

On Thursday, February 7, she called Jillian Becker and asked if she and the children could come over. Plath felt terrible and needed to be with someone. Plath went to the Beckers' and decided she would rather stay there for the night, but she stayed until Sunday evening. The Beckers' offered to get provisions from her flat. She gave Jillian instructions on what she wanted for herself and her children. The Beckers looked after Plath that night. Plath talked about Hughes; as Becker was sitting with Plath waiting for the sleeping pills to take affect, Plath said, "It would be good to get the children away to the seaside. Somewhere warm. They haven't been well. I wish I could take them to Spain." (Becker, 5–6) The next morning, after Plath called Dr. Horder to see if a hospital bed was available, he asked if he could speak with Jillian. He insisted that Plath must take her pills and he was by now sure Plath needed hospitalization. Plath did need help; Dr. Horder encouraged Jillian to let Plath look after Frieda and Nicholas. However, Jillian ended up taking care of them, as Plath was too depressed to do much more than watch.

Over the weekend, Plath met Hughes at her flat, most likely on Saturday. She was exhausted. Frieda regularly woke up crying, asking where her father was, and Hughes missed his daughter just as much. On this night, Plath broke down crying in front of him, saying she wanted to get back together and did not want a divorce. "The collapse of her hard-won facade of proud independence roused all his old tenderness. This must have been 'the most important meeting of my life', which she mentioned to Suzette [Macedo] ... saying 'It's all falling into place. Everything's going to be all right.'" (Feinstein, 141) On Sunday afternoon, February 10, she ate a big dinner and seemed much happier. She fed Nicholas and, then, after a nap, began to briskly gather her things together. "She seemed invigorated, mildly elated, as I'd seldom if ever seen her before." (Becker, 10) Plath wanted to go home, as she said she had to prepare for the week—on Monday a new live-in nanny was due to arrive in the morning, and she had a lunch meeting with David Machin, an editor at Heinemann. Jillian was worried, but let Plath go, having become tired of constantly having to look after her and her children, as well as run her own household. Gerry Becker drove her home, but stopped the old taxi he drove at one point because Plath was crying; he offered to take her back to his home, but Plath replied, "No, this is nonsense, take no notice. I have to get home." (Becker, 12)

Plath returned to 23 Fitzroy Road that evening. Dr. Horder called in on Plath to see if she was all right. Later, she went down to her neighbor, Trevor Thomas, to see if he had any stamps she could purchase because she had a letter addressed to her mother. After this transaction took place, and she insisted on paying him, she asked when he left in the morning. Plath did not move once he had shut his door. Several minutes later, Thomas opened his door and saw Plath standing there as if in a trance. He asked her if she was feeling well, and she said was dreaming.[19] She was still taking antidepressants and her speech was slurred. Thomas offered to call Dr. Horder, but she told him not to, that she would be fine. Deep into the night, Thomas heard Plath pacing around her flat, which eventually subsided.

The next morning, the new nanny, Myra Norris, arrived. She smelled gas, and no one answered the door. She phoned, after the obligatory wait at the phone box, to make sure she had the right address, and was told she did. Norris ran into a builder working on the house and once they were both inside the front door, the smell of the gas was overwhelming. Together they broke into Plath's flat, and found her on the kitchen floor, with Frieda and Nicholas upstairs, sealed in their room with the window open, and a tray with bread and milk by their side. One of Plath's last actions was to seal her children safely in their room. She had left a note on her pram in the main hallway that read, 'Call Dr. Horder'. Artificial respiration failed and Dr. Horder pronounced Plath dead. The antidepressants had given her energy without lifting her spirits, and in her depression, she had killed herself. Plath was thirty years old.

Plath died from gas poisoning, though it was reported in the Wellesley's *Townsman* that she died from viral pneumonia. An inquest of her death was held at the Coroner's Court, St. Pancras Hospital. The funeral for Sylvia Plath took place on February 16, 1963, at St. Thomas à Beckett Church in Heptonstall; Warren and his wife Margaret flew over to attend. Aurelia, told her daughter died of pneumonia, was too shattered and did not attend. Sylvia Plath was buried in the new cemetery at the far side from the church. The inscription on her headstone reads:

IN MEMORY
SYLVIA PLATH HUGHES
1932–1963
EVEN AMIDST FIERCE FLAMES
THE GOLDEN LOTUS CAN BE PLANTED

From atop Scout Rock, a favorite childhood stomping ground of Hughes's several miles to the east in Mytholmroyd, the church tower at Heptonstall can be seen; Sylvia Plath's headstone faces east.

# CHAPTER EIGHT

# The Afterlife of Sylvia Plath

*Writing is a religious act: it is an ordering, a reforming, a relearning ... a shaping which does not pass away like a day....The writing lasts: it goes about on its own in the world. People read it: react to it as to a person, a philosophy, a religion, a flower: they like it, or do not.*

—Sylvia Plath, *Journals*

THE POSTHUMOUS PUBLICATIONS of Sylvia Plath's work and some of the industry's history and controversy require some discussion. There are three major categories that these works can be placed into: poetry, prose, and non-fiction.[1] Although Sylvia Plath has become one of the most celebrated poets in history, her words, life, and legacy have been intensely debated and fiercely guarded. The Estate of Sylvia Plath ("The Estate"), once governed by Ted Hughes, has also been controlled by his sister, Olwyn Hughes, and currently by Plath's children, Frieda and Nicholas. Plath wrote poems to be published; she wanted to be recognized. The fame and recognition she has had following her death has been astronomical. As discussed in the Introduction, Plath's literary importance has steadily risen through the decades. In fact, each time she seems to reach a plateau, there is a publication or discovery to keep her name circulating. There have been far too many biographies, critical essays, and reviews to speak about here in depth, but the Works Cited and Further Reading that follow list the most important publications. Discussion of Ted Hughes's poetry collection, *Birthday Letters*, and his death, both major events in 1998, must be included in order to understand perceptions of Plath after her death.

Though Plath and Hughes were separated at the time of her suicide, they were not divorced and he was left in control of her entire estate.[2] Throughout their marriage, Plath had faithfully and willingly assisted Hughes in preparing his manuscripts for submission and publication. For a time she even responded to some of his mail. Now it was Hughes's responsibility to see that Plath's work remained in circulation. He found her lists of poetry submissions and on March 12, 1963, performed his first deed as executor of her estate by sending some of her newer poems from the previous autumn and late January to the *Critical Quarterly* and the *New Statesman*.[3] Hughes was familiar with Plath's desk and organizational system; he found the manuscript for *Ariel*, along with the late January and early February poems. Plath never mailed the letter(s) she wrote before her death, which occasioned her visit to Trevor Thomas the night before to buy stamps. At some later point, Aurelia Plath denied her right to see the letter, and its whereabouts is not known. (Hayman, 18–19)

Anne Stevenson was commissioned to write the authorized biography of Sylvia Plath.[4] Stevenson was given a large advance to complete the project as well as the cooperation of the Estate with regard to Plath's published and unpublished manuscripts. In 1989, when *Bitter Fame* was published, Stevenson credited Olwyn Hughes as coauthor. This singular confession has tainted the reading for many because Plath herself believed that Olwyn Hughes felt unkindly toward or ambivalently about her. In an interview for the *Observer*, Stevenson discussed the aim of writing the biography. In answer to the comment that *Bitter Fame* reports a number of negative views of Plath, Stevenson said, "[W]ith Olwyn's help I've tried to show as many facets to Plath's life as possible". (Nault, *Observer*) The book also featured three memoirs by

Plath's acquaintances Lucas Myers, Dido Merwin, and Richard Murphy. The inclusion of these memoirs is unusual because their collective tone is not at all celebratory. Each person relates their impressions of Plath and, ultimately, their reservations regarding her behavior and the suitability of her marriage to Hughes.[5]

Coinciding with the publication of *Bitter Fame*, a fierce debate over Sylvia Plath's headstone took place in the London newspapers, *The Guardian* and *The Independent*. Between April 7 and April 24, many letters were printed about Plath's missing headstone, including two long letters by Hughes. It was reported that vandals, deemed the work of angry feminists, had chiseled off the "Hughes" on her grave marker and that the marker had been previously disrespected four times.[6] Through the intense exchange of letters to the editor, the controversy surrounding Sylvia Plath and Ted Hughes was again aroused. There has been no further reported vandalizing of Sylvia Plath's gravestone since it was re-erected on April 29, 1989.

## POSTHUMOUS PUBLICATIONS BY SYLVIA PLATH: THE POETRY

A. Alvarez published a small epitaph along with "Edge," "The Fearful," "Kindness," and "Contusion" on February 17, 1963, in the *Observer*. Alvarez, always supportive of Plath's poetry, wrote one of only a few obituaries for her. In "A Poet's Epitaph," Alvarez declared with assurance that Plath's poetry "represents a totally new breakthrough in modern verse." (Alvarez, *Observer*, 23). He also wrote, "it was only recently that the peculiar intensity of her genius found its perfect expression." (Alvarez, *Observer*, 23) That "perfect expression," undeniably attributed to her poetry, hinted also at Plath's death. In the April issue of *London Magazine*, an additional six poems were printed. In all, more than forty of Plath's last poems, and some prose pieces, were printed in 1963, making it far and away her most successful year.

The 1963 publishing frenzy seemed to be priming the public for a collection of poems. When *Ariel* was published in England on March 11, 1965, reprints were needed at once. By 1981, *Ariel* had sold more than 170,000 copies in England, an extraordinary figure for a collection of poetry.[7] In 1981, Hughes revealed in the

"Notes" section of Plath's *Collected Poems* that the order of the poems in the edition of *Ariel* he published was not the way Plath had prepared the manuscript.[8] Plath's manuscript began with the word "love" and ended with "spring." The order and selection of poems was changed to suit the tastes of the publishers, namely his publisher Faber and Faber. As with the publication of *The Colossus*, when *Ariel* was released the following year in the United States, it contained a slightly different table of contents.[9] Regardless, Plath's reputation was established. The inclusion of a foreword written by Robert Lowell, the leading poet in the United States at the time, furthered the collection's great reception.

Reviews of *Ariel* appeared in a wide variety of periodicals. Robert Lowell's foreword to the edition dealt what could be considered a major blow to Plath's posthumous fame and reputation. Lowell described the poems as "playing Russian roulette with six cartridges in the cylinder." (Lowell, viii) His foreword concluded with his memory of Plath from the time she audited his class at Boston University in 1959, she was "willowy, long-waisted, sharp-elbowed, nervous, giggly, gracious ... Somehow none of it sank very deep into my awareness. I sensed her abashment and distinction, and never guessed her later appalling and triumphant fulfillment" (Lowell, ix).

Alvarez's "perfect expression" and Lowell's "triumphant fulfillment" seem to be aimed specifically at her death, as though Plath's suicide was a result of her poetry. One need only consider the tender poems Plath wrote about her children to understand more fully the complexity of the major themes and emotions prevailing in her late poetry. Furthermore, suggesting that the poetry Sylvia Plath wrote caused her to commit suicide discredits the actual accomplishments that her oeuvre exhibits.

After *Ariel* was published, Plath's poetry and prose appeared somewhat sporadically over the next two decades. However, more than twenty poems appeared in periodicals between 1970 and 1971. Most of these poems were then collected and published in either *Crossing the Water: Transitional Poems* or *Winter Trees: Late Poems*, both published in 1971 immediately after *The Bell Jar* was published in the United States.[10] The poems in these collections were primarily written by Plath between 1960 and 1962, and many of them were published during her lifetime. The editions contained noticeably different tables of contents on either side of the Atlantic. For example, the American edition of *Crossing the Water* printed a majority of the poems included in Heinemann's 1960 edition of *The Colossus*, which were excluded from Knopf's 1962 edition. In addition to the more mass produced collections, a wide variety of poems, spanning nearly all of Plath's professional writing, were also printed in limited editions by smaller presses throughout the 1970s. In all, Hughes oversaw the publication of more than a dozen of these editions of both poetry and prose.

The *Times Literary Supplement* reviewed both *Crossing the Water* and *Winter Trees* in December 1971. According to the anonymous reviewer, "The latest poems ... were written at a time when Sylvia Plath had stepped away from the traceable influences of her first book into a discovery of a style—more specifically, a vocabulary—which, in the earlier work, was always on the verge of being liberated." (*Times Literary Supplement,* 1602) Simply put, the poems in *The Colossus* merely hinted at the significant work the author would go on to produce. They also wondered "how many more poems are yet to come, and from which period."

*The Collected Poems* of Sylvia Plath was published in 1981. It is not too surprising that the *Collected Poems* was the winner of the 1982 Pulitzer Prize. The volume shows the short but amazing progression of Plath's poetry from 1956 to 1963, her time at Cambridge to her death in London. When Hughes published *Crossing the Water* and *Winter Trees*, he filled in the large gap, which was Plath's poetic progression. At the back of the collection, a list of Plath's "Juvenilia" was printed, which included nearly all of her pre-1956 poetry. A selected fifty were printed in full.[11] The evolution of her style, voice, and her apparent willingness to go deeper into subject matter grew parallel with her daily life. Sylvia Plath had won awards throughout her life; even though she had been deceased for nineteen years, the Pulitzer Prize seemed to be a fitting honor.

Plath also wrote three long children's poems, none of which were included in the *Collected Poems*. The poems, published as *The*

*Bed Book, The It-Doesn't-Matter Suit,* and *Mrs. Cherry's Kitchen,* show a severely ignored aspect to Plath's writing: playfulness. Ironically, all three stories were written prior to her own children being born, with only *The Bed Book* being written during her first pregnancy in 1959. She has been commonly viewed as a dark and depressing writer, void of any signs of happiness; but, evidently, with regard to these poems, this cannot be considered accurate.

## THE PROSE

Unlike most books, *The Bell Jar* had three separate, significant publications. The first in 1963 (discussed briefly in the prior chapter), another in 1966, and the third, and largest, in 1971. When it was published for the first time in January 1963, reviews showed admiration for the skill 'Victoria Lucas' displayed handling such an emotional subject. Ruby Millar acknowledged, "This experience is described with absolute ruthlessness, yet with humour." (Millar, 17) Perhaps Plath attempted to out-Salinger Salinger since *The Bell Jar* explores similar themes as J.D. Salinger's *The Catcher in the Rye,* published in 1951. Both involve young adults in New York City trying to cope with social issues, maturity, and descending depressions. Plath also admitted to admiring Mary Jane Ward's novel, *The Snake Pit,* which dealt with mental illness, too.

Less than six weeks after Plath's death, Hughes gave Heinemann permission to disclose her identity as the author of *The Bell Jar.* As a poet, Plath had decided in 1961 that she wanted anonymity; she did not want her fiction to be judged as the work of a poet. An edition of *The Bell Jar* was already slated for release in September 1964 by Contemporary Fiction, a subsidiary of William Heinemann Limited. On the back of this book it states that "Victoria Lucas" was a pseudonym, but they did not disclose the author's identity at that time. Faber issued the first edition of *The Bell Jar* that appeared with Plath listed as the author and released it in September, 1966. Upon its second release in 1966, reviews were more prominent and promising. In one review, Valerie Pitt praised *The Bell Jar* for being "a poetic novel" and that there was enough merit found in it "to make one regret, increasingly, the early death not

only of so brilliant a writer but of so uncommon a personality."
(Pitt, 11) *The Bell Jar* was finally published in the United States in
1971, and it was an instant national bestseller, remaining atop the
best-seller list for nearly six months. The reviews and attention
*The Bell Jar* received at this release would skyrocket the novel into
a rare, mythic category of modern fiction. It has also become a
Book-of-the-Month Club selection, as well as a fixture on high
school reading lists. Though many of the social barriers that
plagued Esther Greenwood have been removed, teenage girls
around the world still face the same kind of confusion in their
own coming-of-age struggles.

Plath worked diligently to get to the stage when she could write
a novel. Just as some of her early poems pave a route leading to
*Ariel,* the stories Plath wrote experimented with voice and led to
*The Bell Jar.* A short story collection titled, *Johnny Panic and the
Bible of Dreams* was published in 1977 and received rather quietly. The title is taken from a story Plath wrote in Boston in 1959
about her experience working at the Massachusetts General Hospital typing patient records in the psychiatric ward. *Johnny Panic*
contains a great mixture of Plath's prose writing from her early
apprentice years to the more mature stories written in the late
1950s. It also printed, for the first time, sections from her private
journals. Margaret Atwood points out that *Johnny Panic* is rich
for the reader interested in "foreshadowings, cross-references,
influences and insights." (Atwood, 10) Ted Hughes wrote separate introductions for the editions published in the United
Kingdom and the United States, each varying in length and content, but solid in authenticity. Ultimately, Hughes believed Plath
would always be known as a poet; he wrote, "It is strange that she
was so much more patient with her poems." (*Johnny Panic,* 4) He
was not as approving of Plath's endeavors in short fiction as he
was of her poetry, but he does admit to being "more inclined to
think any bit of evidence which corrects and clarifies our idea of
what she really was is important, insofar as her writings persuade
us of her importance," which is why he opted to edit the collection. (*Johnny Panic,* 8)

## PLATH'S NON-FICTION

After the somewhat debased emotions portrayed in *The Bell Jar*, Aurelia Plath sought to correct her image, and the image of her family, by reproducing Plath's letters. (Feinstein, 184) *Letters Home* was published in the United States in 1975 (it was published the following year in England) and received mixed reviews between the two countries. Mrs. Plath was hoping it would serve as a corrective to the portrayal and caricature the family was given in *The Bell Jar*.[12] The letters selected for publication represented only Plath's side of the story, but Aurelia explained her side through a long introduction and some commentary interspersed throughout. *The New Yorker* balanced all the known facts and reported that Plath, "... always tried too hard, never allowed herself any margin for failure, and never forgave herself for less than perfection" and that "many of her other characteristics were life-preserving. Enthusiasm, generosity, curiosity, lovingness, and kindness are on the list." (*New Yorker* 51 [Dec. 1975], 95–96) They concluded that Plath's death was tragic, not her life. Peter Ackroyd, in *Spectator*, finds so much to criticize in his review, "Dear Mummy, I hate you." Ackroyd concludes "the letters are so unrevealing about the life ..." he feels Plath's fame had ended. (Ackroyd, 21) However, *Letters Homes* is a tasteful collection. Its importance may grow over time, necessitating a complete edition in the future.

After publishing *Letters Home*, and after preparing a selection of Plath's journals for publication in the *Johnny Panic* collection, the Estate planned to publish a larger selection of Plath's private journals. In 1982, *The Journals of Sylvia Plath* met with even more criticism than any other Plath book to date. Ted Hughes acted as consulting editor for the edition and also wrote the foreword. Plath's journals, in conjunction with her letters, act as the unofficial autobiography of her last thirteen years. Both publications commence in 1950. Reviews of the *Journals* questioned the appropriateness of publishing such private material and further questioned the omissions. Hughes published a longer foreword in *Grand Street*, which he had intended to see in print in the *Journals*. In both forewords, he admits to destroying Plath's last journal and misplacing the preceding one, hopeful it would be found. (*Journals* [1982], xiii) The *Journals*, though, are an important resource for readers of Sylvia Plath, and they were only published in the United States.

Copies of the American edition of the *Journals* appeared in England, though; they could be found in used bookshops, market stalls, and occasionally in retail shops. In February, 1998, Ted Hughes and the Estate authorized Karen V. Kukil, Associate Curator of Rare Books at Smith College, to begin editing an unabridged edition. It would mark the first time Plath's journals would appear in the United Kingdom. Smith College purchased Plath's journals, as well as the manuscripts for the *Ariel* poems, and many other items, in the early 1980s. Several of the journals, however, were sealed by Hughes until just before he died in 1998. A few weeks before the official publication date of April 1, 2000, *The Guardian* began to serialize extracts of the book.[13] Katharine Viner, literary critic for *The Guardian* wrote, "The journals reveal, more than anything, a woman in conflict." (*Guardian*) Viner also points out that a contradiction exists between some of the newly revealed journal entries and the corresponding letters that Plath was writing about and to her mother. Collectively, now, the letters and the journals combine to make an extraordinary life history. This publication was a major literary event; across the board, reviewers of these *Journals* were pleased.

## BIRTHDAY LETTERS AND THE DEATH OF TED HUGHES

Ted Hughes secretly wrote poems of remembrance of his courtship, marriage, life, and afterlife with Plath and published them, quite unexpectedly, in *Birthday Letters*.[14] The *Times of London* began serialization of them on January 17, 1998. Hughes had maintained a committed silence about his marriage to Plath for over three decades. He hoped the silence would prevent too much intrusion by the public into his private life; it had the exact opposite effect. It has proven difficult not to read the poems in *Birthday Letters*, which were his first words about Plath, biographically. He colored some of his memories with poetic license, just as Plath had done in a few of her poems about him.[15] The poems were such a departure from Hughes's previous writing that they were deemed more authentic. The collection was received favorably in both the United Kingdom and the United States.[16]

The interest in *Birthday Letters* sparked great debate. "The Sylvia Plath Forum," moderated by Elaine Connell and Chris Ratcliffe in Hebden Bridge, Yorkshire, started online almost immediately after the poems were printed in England.[17] Connell said:

> My decision to start the Forum was prompted by the publication of Birthday Letters. It had been in my mind for a couple of months beforehand but [Birthday Letters] provided a spur as it was so unexpected and its contents were so revelatory ... But even though I had a more sympathetic approach to him than most other feminists I was still surprised by the depth of the love he displayed and the sense of the loss he had experienced ... " (Connell, letter)

Initially, the Forum sought to moderate a discussion of *Birthday Letters*, Ted Hughes, and Sylvia Plath, but it has developed into the largest and most popular online resource about Plath. The forum has been a very energetic meeting ground for beginners in Sylvia Plath study and published scholars, such as Connell, Judith Kroll, Kate Moses, and Lynda K. Bundtzen.

Ted Hughes died on October 28, 1998, in England; he was sixty-eight. Hughes had contracted colon cancer and, not surprisingly, kept it a secret. His passing made the front pages of newspapers worldwide and was a huge loss to literature. Poets and those who knew him mourned the loss of the most powerful poet of the twentieth century in England. Shortly after his death, the *Daily Telegraph* printed an interview with Hughes conducted by Eilat Negev in 1996. Those who wondered why Hughes published *Birthday Letters* were made aware of Hughes's reasons for silence. Hughes had begun to write poems about Plath in order to achieve some release from her death.

ON JULY 28, 2000, the English Heritage acknowledged Plath's important contribution to literature and her staying power by adding a blue plaque at 3 Chalcot Square. From a literary viewpoint, this is one of the highest honors bestowed on a deceased writer. The English Heritage statement of the blue plaque's presence and purpose is to commemorate the association between a person and a building. Consideration for a blue plaque for Plath was given because she had been deceased longer than twenty years, the minimum time required. The building must still exist, and a person may only receive one plaque.[1] Frieda Hughes, who was born in the house in 1960, and Nicholas Hughes were both at the small ceremony to unveil the plaque on the house.

In several letters to the editor regarding the placement of the plaque, many wondered why a blue plaque was not added to W.B. Yeats' residence at 23 Fitzroy Road. It has often been misunderstood that the poems Plath is known for were not written in Yeats' house. She did write a dozen poems there, but the fact that her suicide also took place there made the Chalcot Square location more appropriate. In a letter to the editor in *The Times of London,* Frieda Hughes defended the blue plaque's placement at 3 Chalcot Square, also admitting that, "more than anyone else I celebrate her life and the life she gave me." (July 31, 2000)

In the autumn of 2002, Kathleen Connors and Indiana University, Bloomington hosted "The Art of Sylvia Plath." The project featured a commemorative concert, a literary symposium, and for the first time, an original artwork exhibit by Plath. The concert featured music by the Pulitzer Prize winning composer, Shulamit

Ran. Diane Middlebrook presented on the legendary creative union between Plath and Hughes.[2]

The Sylvia Plath 70th Year Literary Symposium spanned four days. Among the featured speakers were Lynda K. Bundtzen (author of *Plath's Incarnations* and *The Other Ariel*), Judith Kroll (author of *Chapters in a Mythology*), Tracy Brain (author of *The Other Sylvia Plath*), Robin Peel (author of *Writing Back*), Kate Moses (author of *Wintering*), and Susan van Dyne (author of *Revising Life*). The symposium included students and scholars from many different countries who presented papers and discussed various topics and issues. Subjects ranged from motherhood to feminism, and "Plath as Icon" to her "Language/Literary Expression."

In conjunction with the symposium, Indiana University also held "Eye Rhymes: Visual Art and Manuscripts of Sylvia Plath." The exhibit featured various art works by Plath spanning nearly her whole life, as well as memorabilia, such as her passport and scrapbooks. The exhibit included materials held in the archives of the Lilly Library and Smith College. It also explored, for the first time, the interconnectedness between Plath's poetry and art. Starting at a very early age, Plath had an eye for detail that would later manifest itself more successfully in poetry.

Although Sylvia Plath has been dead for more than forty years, her hold on the reader has never been stronger. She has been continually "patched, retreaded and approved for the road." (*The Bell Jar*, 275) Her poems, journals, letters, fiction, nonfiction, and art provide the reader with the most important facts of her life. Plath has progressed through the decades by dominating attention in poetry and biography. She is now ageless.

## ACKNOWLEDGMENTS

I am deeply grateful for the following authors for their work on Sylvia Plath: Lena A. Friesen, Elaine Connell, Robin Peel, Tracy Brain, Lynda K. Bundtzen, A. Alvarez, Mary Lynn Broe, Nancy Hargrove, Tim Kendall, Janet Malcolm, Diane Middlebrook, Kate Moses, Charles Newman, Anne Stevenson, and Linda Wagner-Martin.

I am immensely thankful for the invaluable assistance of Barbara Blumenthal, Karen Kukil and the staff of the Mortimer Rare Book Room, Neilson Library, Smith College as well as Becky Cape and staff at the Lilly Library, Indiana University, with the respective Sylvia Plath archives.

## INTRODUCTION

1. Knopf published the first United States edition of *The Colossus* in May 1962.
2. Faber published the first edition of *The Bell Jar* to appear with Plath's name as the author in 1966.
3. *The Guardian*, April 4, 2000, published an article by Stephen Moss titled "The longest suicide note eve written?"
4. *Ted Hughes: A Life* by Elaine Feinstein and *Her Husband* by Diane Middlebrook were published in 2001 and 2003, respectively.

## CHAPTER 1: BECOMING A POET

1. Paul Alexander provided valuable research into the origins of Otto Plath's family in his biography *Rough Magic*.
2. http://users.ev1.net/~Jdavies/Genealogy/Voigt.txt
3. http://www.geocities.com/jphistoricalsociety/plath.html
4. http://www.arboretum.harvard.edu/aboutus/history.html
5. The E.B. Newton School is a registered historical building in Winthrop. A sign in front of the school, seen in April 2003, mentioned Sylvia Plath as a former attendee of the school.
6. Sylvia Plath's unpublished Journals, July 24, 1947–March 25, 1948, The Lilly Library, Indiana University.
7. *Writing Back: Sylvia Plath and Cold War Politics* by Robin Peel was published in 2002. It is the first book-length study to concentrate on Plath's political writing and attitude. It is an important contribution to Plath studies.
8. Sylvia Plath, "Sarah," unpublished short story, The Lilly Library, Indiana University.
9. "Mature," in this instance, is a relative term. The decision to publish her journals starting with 1950 possibly coincides with Plath's going away to college that same year.

## CHAPTER 2: CLIMBING THE RANKS: PLATH AT SMITH

1. See Plath's *Unabridged Journals*, page 36, entry 40 and page 44, entry 48.
2. The name 'Emile' causes immediate pause as her father's middle name was Emil.
3. On the copy held at the Mortimer Rare Book Room, Smith College, there is a handwritten date of "July 19, 1955" next to Plath's name and her Wellesley address. "Tea With Olive Higgins Prouty" remains unpublished.
4. Plath's first roommate, Ann Davidow, left Smith after nearly having a breakdown because she found Smith too difficult. Plath missed Davidow and they kept in contact up until Plath's death in 1963.
5. Compare pages 51–52, entry 58 in the *Unabridged Journals* to the last scene of Chapter Five in *The Bell Jar*.
6. These letters are held at the Lilly Library, Indiana University.
7. Plath loathed her required course in chemistry. She would eventually, successfully, get it changed for a course on Milton.
8. Richard Norton's letters during this period are held at the Lilly Library, Indiana University.
9. In December 1952, Plath and Lotz went on a date and walked by the Northampton mental hospital nearby Smith, and Plath wrote to her mother: "I want so badly to *learn* about *why* and *how* people cross the borderline between sanity and insanity!" (*Letters Home*, 100)

## CHAPTER 3: THE WORLD SPLIT OPEN

1. Indiana University holds Plath's *Mademoiselle* papers from this summer. Much of the following information was taken from these notes on a research visit made from September 1–7, 2003.
2. The Barbizon is now called The Melrose. Plath's room, room 1511, no longer exists.
3. Letter from Sylvia Plath to her mother, dated June 3, 1953, held at the Lilly Library, Indiana University.
4. Letter from Marybeth Little to Sylvia Plath, dated May 5, 1953.
5. See *Boston Globe* archives for August 25 through August 27, 1953. *The Boston Herald* also ran stories on the same days.
6. *The Dybbuk* began a revival run at the Fourth Street Theater in 1954.

## CHAPTER 4: PLATH IN ENGLAND

1. Plath wrote a short story titled "The Matisse Chapel" based on her visit to Vence. The story was not published during her lifetime and is currently uncollected.
2. Falcon Yard was located up from Market Hill off Petty Cury. It was demolished during the winter of 1997.
3. "An American in Paris" appeared on April 21, "Smith College in Retrospect" appeared on May 12, and "May Week Fashions" appeared on

May 26, 1956. Only "May Week Fashions" has been reprinted; it appeared on pages 236–7 in *Letters Home*.

4. This collection has come to be known as the "Cambridge Manuscript" and it was returned to Ted Hughes after its discovery. The news was printed in the *Times of London* on December 17, 1968.

## CHAPTER 5: EXPLORATIONS IN AMERICA

1. See *Journals*, pages 304 and 320. Plath titled her story "Changeabout [*sic*] in Mrs. Cherry's Kitchen," but when the story was published in 2001, by Faber and Faber, as Plath's *Collected Children's Stories*, it was simply called *Mrs. Cherry's Kitchen*.

2. Rich remembers Plath asking her about combining writing and motherhood, and Rich recalls her reply: "'I answered something very sage, like 'It can be done, but you'd better think about it really hard.'" (Middlebrook, 111)

3. *Journals*, 392. On the night of their first meeting, Plath bit Hughes, marking him. See *Journals*, page 212. The first night Plath and Hughes spent together left her bruised. See *Journals*, page 552.

4. This style of writing was much favored by Marianne Moore, a large influence on Plath at this time.

5. *The New Yorker* re-titled it as "Night Walk"; in Plath's *Collected Poems* it appears as "Hardcastle Crags."

6. In a letter to her mother, Plath explained that "When asked, 'Why the Lorelei,' he said they were my 'own kin.' I was quite amazed." (*Letters Home*, 346) The legend of the Lorelei is Germanic. At a particular spot on the River Rhine in Germany, the Lorelei would sing from dusk till dawn. The sweetness of the song misleads the men driving boats, often fatally harming those that listened and sought to find them.

7. Both Acorn Street and Louisburg Square are considered to be among the most exclusive streets in the United States. Additionally, Acorn Street is possibly the most photographed street in the United States.

8. For a complete history of Scollay Square read David Kruh's excellent *Always Something Doing*. Scollay Square was obliterated during the 1960s in favor of a government building and windswept plaza.

9. Ironically, this stolen pink paper was returned to Smith College, for a price, in the 1980s when they purchased her papers from the Estate of Sylvia Plath.

10. In her largely autobiographical *The Bell Jar*, Esther visits her father's grave; it is not known if Plath did this in August 1953.

11. It was not uncommon for her to go 35–40 days or more between periods.

## CHAPTER 6: CONFINED SPACES

1. After Plath's death, Hughes destroyed one of the journals and later misplaced another one.

2. Hughes began giving lists of poetry subjects to Plath shortly after their marriage.
3. Many of the sums of money Plath and Hughes were receiving may not appear to be much, but in the 1950s and 1960s, any amount of money they received, such as £500, was considered a large sum.
4. For careful considerations of Plath's political writing and awareness read *The Other Sylvia Plath* by Tracy Brain and *Writing Back: Sylvia Plath and Cold War Politics* by Robin Peel.
5. *The Observer* did not publish poems every week, but when they did, they usually appeared in the "Arts" section. Plath's "Poem" appeared on page 22. In *The Savage God*, Alvarez remembered receiving the poems and finding "Night Shift" unusually accomplished. See pages 23–24 in "Prologue: Sylvia Plath."
6. Plath was always homesick for one beach in particular: "My favorite beach in the world is Nauset, and my heart aches for it." (*Letters Home*, 391)
7. Plath had taught Lawrence's novel while at Smith, using photocopies.
8. This verdict was, in a way, a freeing act for all writers in the United Kingdom, not just the deceased Lawrence.
9. Emory University, Atlanta, Georgia, purchased papers from Ted Hughes. Some of the papers are manuscripts of Plath's work.
10. Letter to Ann Goodman dated April 27, 1961.
11. *ibid.*
12. See the poem "Stubbing Wharfe," page 106–8, in Ted Hughes's *Birthday Letters* collection. The pub, Stubbing Wharf is just west of Hebden Bridge center, far below the hilltop village of Heptonstall. According to the poem, they visited the pub in December 1959 upon returning to England.

CHAPTER 7: THE TRIUMPHANT FULFILLMENT

1. http://freepages.genealogy.rootsweb.com/~footprints1/dev1/northtawton/homepage.htm
2. Hughes discussed his reaction to "The Moon and the Yew Tree" in his "Notes on the Chronological Order of Sylvia Plath's Poems" first published in *TriQuarterly* 7, Fall 1966.
3. Plath's reputation was high enough that she was asked to be a judge for the Guinness prizes in 1962.
4. *Letters Home*, pg. 436. Reference to this acceptance and publication can be found in Letters Home. In particular, in Plath's letters written between September–November, 1961 on pages 430, 431, 432, 434, 435, and 436. Lena A. Friesen, a Plath scholar, pointed out the reference to me in December 2001. In the letter dated November 9, 1961, Plath writes of receiving a fan letter for her story, specifically mentioning Whitby and Canada. At Smith College, in January 2002, I found a typed manuscript of a story that takes place in Whitby, England, and has a character from Canada. This story is entitled "The Lucky Stone." Written at the top of one draft, in Plath's hand,

is "Sold £15.15.0 by Jennifer Hassell." The address typed at the top right hand corner of the first page is 3 Chalcot Square, London NW1. Smith also owns a letter from an editor at *My Weekly*, dated January 19, 1962, rejecting two of Plath's stories. In the letter, the editor encourages Plath to send in more stories for consideration, commenting that the magazine did enjoy "The Lucky Stone." There are various editorial changes between Plath's typed manuscript and the published story, including a titled change to "The Perfect Place." The story appeared in the October 28, 1961 issue of *My Weekly*. Without Ms. Friesen, and the indispensable help of Irralie Doel, of Liverpool University, the discovery of this short story and its publication history might not have ever been made. The original source of notification of acceptance from Jennifer Hassell, if it exists, has not been found. The fan letter, which has not yet been located, is presumably lost.

5. After one meeting in early March, Plath broke down in tears, afraid that her Americanisms were being misinterpreted by the English. See *Journals*, pg. 636–7.

6. Laura Riding, an American poet, had lived with Robert Graves and inspired his book, *The White Goddess*, a large influence on Plath and Hughes. See *Writing Back* by Robin Peel for more information.

7. *The New Yorker* printed "The Elm Speaks" and six other poems after Plath's death on August 3, 1963.

8. Smith College holds a note saying the Knopf edition of *The Colossus* had a net loss of $1,420.

9. Elizabeth wrote to the Hughes in 1961, after hearing them complain on the BBC about their lack of space in London, offering them retreat at her country home for space and quiet.

10. Eilat Negev, speaking at the Sylvia Plath 70th Year Symposium in October 2002, revealed that based on interviews she conducted, that Hughes had actually gone to Spain with Assia Wevill.

11. O'Neill-Roe was found by Davies on Aurelia's request.

12. In "Ariel," Plath describes the horse's eye as "Nigger-eye." There has been some controversy over Plath's usage of the word "Nigger" here, but it is used in a purely adjectival sense for the word 'black.' In the original draft of the poem, Plath used 'blackberries' rather than 'berries.' She had already written and published her poem "Blackberrying," so in this sense it is a variation of a theme.

13. Ariel, as a character in Shakespeare's *The Tempest*, is set free by his master Prospero at the end of the play; Ariel was also the singer of "Full Fathom Five," a title from Plath's 1958 poem.

14. Lately Plath had been corresponding with Father Michael, an American Catholic priest visiting Oxford; he was writing poems and sent his to Plath to be critiqued. She in turn asked him to bless her, even though she was not one of the faithful.

15. Plath paraphrased a quote from Yeats's play, *The Unicorn and the Stars*. The actual quote is:

"Go, then, get food and drink, whatever is wanted to give you strength and courage. Gather your people together here, bring them in. We have a great thing to do, I have to begin—I want to tell it to the whole world. Bring them in, bring them in, I will make the house ready." (Yeats, 347)

16. Knopf rejected it once they learned that "Victoria Lucas" was actually Sylvia Plath. Ironically, Knopf sent Plath a letter in 1952 after reading "Sunday at the Mintons'" encouraging her to submit a novel to them for publication.

17. Plath planned on returning to Court Green in the spring and summer, subletting her new flat while she was away for the other half of the year.

18. These poems, listed in the order Plath has them, are on the last page of her lists held at Smith College. "Contusion" is written in under "Balloons" in Plath's pen. This is circumstantial evidence that "Edge" may not be the last poem Plath wrote. "Edge" seems to me too ironic a choice to conclude the *Collected Poems* and judging from the care in which Plath took to protect her children during her suicide attempt, "Balloons" or "Contusion" may be considered Plath's last poem, but we may never know for sure what her last poem was.

19. Trevor Thomas's memoirs, *Last Encounters* was self-published in 1987. A copy is held at the Mortimer Rare Book Room at Smith College.

## CHAPTER 8: THE AFTERLIFE OF SYLVIA PLATH

1. Another interesting segment in the publishing history of Sylvia Plath is how her work has been marketed over the years. Tracy Brain has written an excellent account of the industry in "Packaging of Sylvia Plath" in *The Other Sylvia Plath*, in Chapter One between pages 1–12.

2. The legal term for this is "intestate."

3. Smith College, "Lists."

4. Plath's biographers include Edward Butscher, Linda Wagner-Martin, Anne Stevenson, Paul Alexander, and Ronald Hayman. The last biography of Sylvia Plath appeared in 1991. Please see the Works Cited and Further Reading for more information.

5. For further reading, please see "The Archive" in *The Haunting of Sylvia Plath* by Jacqueline Rose and *The Silent Woman* by Janet Malcolm.

6. Ted Hughes's "The place where Sylvia Plath should rest is in peace," printed in *The Guardian*, April 20, 1989.

7. All sales figures in this chapter were obtained from Stephen Tabor's *Sylvia Plath: An Analytical Bibliography*.

8. For further reading, see *The Other Ariel* by Lynda K. Bundtzen.

9. This would be the case for each simultaneously published book by Plath until *The Collected Poems* appeared.

10. Winter Trees was actually published in the United States in September 1972.
11. One of Plath's best early poems, "Mad Girl's Love Song," was neither one of the selected nor included in the list.
12. This point-counterpoint publication scheme, where one volume would speak for or try to balance out another can be viewed as such: *Letters Home* was seen as the answer to *The Bell Jar* and later, the *Journals* would answer *Letters Home.*
13. This date was also the fortieth birthday of Frieda Hughes.
14. As it turns out, a number of these poems were printed previously in his *New Selected Poems, 1957–1994.*
15. Erica Wagner, the literary critic for the *Times of London,* published *Ariel's Gift,* the only book-length study of *Birthday Letters* to date.
16. In England, however, the poems were revered to a greater extent and for a longer period of time. Hughes achieved the greatest amount of success since the early 1970s in the United States, when his brilliant poetry collection *Crow* was published.
17. The Sylvia Plath Forum is located on the Internet at http://www.sylvi-aplathforum.com.

## AFTERWORD

1. For more information on the Blue Plaque, and a list of recipients and locations, please visit the English Heritage website, located at http://www.english-heritage.org.uk/.
2. This lecture was expanded upon in Middlebrook's biography *Her Husband: Hughes and Plath—A Marriage.* The book focuses on the writing lives and marriage of Sylvia Plath and Ted Hughes and how the work of one poet influenced the work of the other. The book was published in October 2003.

Ackroyd, Peter. "Dear Mummy, I hate you". *Spectator* (24 Apr. 1976, p. 21).

Alexander, Paul. *Rough Magic: A Biography of Sylvia Plath.* New York: Viking Penguin, 1992.

Alvarez, A. "A Poet's Epitaph". *Observer* (17 Feb. 1963, p. 23).

———. "The Poet and the Poetess" *Observer* (18 Dec. 1960, p.12).

———. *The Savage God: A Study of Suicide.* New York: W. W. Norton, 1990.

Atwood, Margaret. "Poet's Prose". *New York Times Book Review* (28 Jan. 1979, p. 10).

"Beautiful Smith Girl Missing at Wellesley". *Boston Globe* (25 Aug. 1953, pp. 1, 9).

Becker, Jillian. *Giving Up: The Last Days of Sylvia Plath.* London: Ferrington, 2002.

Burroway, Janet. *Embalming Mom.* Iowa City: University of Iowa Press, 2002.

Butscher, Edward, ed. *Sylvia Plath: The Woman & The Work.* New York: Dodd, Mead and Company, 1977.

"College-Age Girl". *Christian Science Monitor* (10 Jul. 1952, p. 15)

Connell, Elaine. Letter to author, 25 July 2003.

"Day-Long Search Fails to Locate Plath Girl". *Boston Globe* (26 Aug. 1953, pp. 1, 11).

Feinstein, Elaine. *Ted Hughes: The Life of a Poet.* London: W.W. Norton, 2001.

Hayman, Ronald. *The Death and Life of Sylvia Plath.* New York: Birch Lane Press, 1991.

Hughes, Frieda. 'Plath's blue plaque'. *The Times of London* (31 July 2000).

Lowell, Robert. Foreword to *Ariel,* by Sylvia Plath. New York: Harper and Row, 1966.

Malcolm, Janet. *The Silent Woman.* New York: Vintage, 1994.

Matovich, Richard M. *A Concordance to the Collected Poems of Sylvia Plath*. New York and London: Garland, 1986.

Middlebrook, Diane Wood. *Anne Sexton: A Biography*. New York: Houghton Mifflin, 1991.

Millar, Ruby. "In the Good Old Days". *Derbyshire Times* (15 Feb. 1963, pg. 17).

Nault, Marianne. "Explorer of the underworld within", interview with Anne Stevenson, *The Observer* (15 Oct. 1989).

Newman, Charles, ed. *The Art of Sylvia Plath: A Symposium*. Bloomington: Indiana University Press, 1970.

*New Yorker* 51 (22 Dec. 1975, pp. 95–6).

Orr, Peter. *The Poet Speaks*. London: Routledge, 1966.

Peril, Lynn. *Pink Think: Becoming a Woman in Many Uneasy Lessons*. New York: W.W. Norton, 2002.

Pitt, Valerie. "Isolated Case". *Sunday Telegraph* (25 Sept. 1966, pg. 11).

Plath, Sylvia. *Ariel*. With a Foreword by Robert Lowell. New York: Harper and Row, 1966.

———. *Collected Poems*. London: Faber and Faber, 1981.

———. *Johnny Panic and the Bible of Dreams*. New York: Harper Colophon, 1980.

———. *Letters Home*, ed. Aurelia Schober Plath. New York: Harper and Row, 1975.

———. "My Garden". *The Phillipian* 19 (Nov. 1957, p. 7).

———. *The Bell Jar*. New York: Harper & Row, 1971.

———. *The Journals of Sylvia Plath*. New York: Dial Press, 1982.

———. *The Journals of Sylvia Plath*, ed. Karen V. Kukil. London: Faber and Faber, 2000.

Plath, Sylvia and Perry Norton. "Youth's Appeal for World Peace." *Christian Science Monitor*, March 16, 1950, 19.

Pochoda, Elizabeth, "The Only Novel of the Dead Poet, Sylvia Plath." *Glamour* (June 1971, p. 119).

Sexton, Anne. *No Evil Star*. Ann Arbor, University of Michigan Press, 1985.

Steiner, Nancy Hunter. *A Closer Look at Ariel*. George Stade, introduction. New York: Harper's Magazine Press, 1973.

Stevenson, Anne. *Bitter Fame: A Life of Sylvia Plath*. New York: Penguin, 1990.

Tabor, Stephen. *Sylvia Plath: An Analytical Bibliography*. Westport, Conn.: Meckler Publishing, 1987.

Viner, Katharine. 'Who was Sylvia?' *Guardian* (18 Mar. 2000, pg. 12).

*Voices & Visions* (poets' series on video). Mystic Fire Video, 1988.

Wagner, Erica. *Ariel's Gift*. London: Faber and Faber, 2000.

'A World in Disintegration'. *Times Literary Supplement* (24 Dec. 1971, pg. 1602).

Yeats, William Butler. *Collected Plays of W. B. Yeats*. London: Macmillan, 1953.

1932    Sylvia Plath is born in Boston's South End on October 27, and lives with her parents Otto and Aurelia at their home in Jamaica Plain neighborhood of Boston at 24 Prince Street.

1934    Otto Plath's landmark book *Bumblebees and Their Ways* is published by the Macmillan Company, New York.

1935    Warren Joseph Plath is born on April 27 in Jamaica Plain, Boston.

1936    The Plaths sell their Jamaica Plain house and move to 92 Johnson Avenue in Winthrop, Massachusetts.

1937    Enrolls in Winthrop's Sunshine School.

1938    Begins the Annie F Warren Grammar School in Winthrop; the Greater Boston area is struck by a fierce hurricane.

1939    Otto Plath slowly becomes ill; Plath begins spending an increased amount of time living with her grandparents at 892 Shirley Street, Winthrop, in a neighborhood called Point Shirley.

1940    Enters Winthrop's E.B. Newton School; she is a star student, achieving straight A's; Otto Plath stubs his toe and develops gangrene; he enters the New England Deaconess Hospital in the Longwood Medical Area, Boston, and has his left, gangrenous leg amputated; on November 5, Otto Plath dies from an embolus in his lung.

1941    Sylvia Plath's "Poem" appears in the *Boston Herald* on August 10, her first professional acceptance.

1942    Aurelia Plath and her parents sell their Winthrop homes and buy a modest white clapboard house at 26 Elmwood Road, Wellesley; Plath repeats fifth grade at the Marshall Perrin Grammar School; the Plath's begin attending the Unitarian Church.

1943–4    Attends Camp Weetamoe in Center Ossipee, New Hampshire.

1944    Enters the Alice L. Phillips Junior High School; begins publishing poems in the school newspapers and writing in a journal.

1945–6    Plath attends Camp Helen Storrow on Buzzard's Bay, Cape Cod.

| 1947 | Attends Vineyard Sailing Camp at Oak Bluffs, Martha's Vineyard; enters Gamaliel Bradford Senior High School in Wellesley; meets her English teacher, Wilbury Crockett, who becomes her mentor and supporter. |
|---|---|
| 1948 | At year-end, Plath is named co-editor of her school newspaper, *The Bradford*; continues academic excellence and recognition, praised for creative writing and artwork. |
| 1949 | Attends Unitarian conference Star Island, off New Hampshire; begins dating several boys at a time. |
| 1950 | Begins publishing articles, and eventually poems, in the *Christian Science Monitor*; accepted into Class of 1954 at Smith College, Northampton, MA; later receives $850 scholarship in the name of Olive Higgins Prouty; *Seventeen* magazine accepts her short story "And Summer Will Not Come Again" for their August issue after nearly fifty rejections; receives fan letter from Eddie Cohen; begins letter correspondence; begins courses at Smith College, resides in Haven House. |
| 1951 | Begins relationship with Richard "Dick" Norton, a senior at Yale University and Wellesley native; attends Yale Junior Prom with Dick Norton; meets Eddie Cohen who drove from Chicago to escort her home during spring vacation; works as a nanny for family in Swampscott, MA. |
| 1952 | Waitresses at The Belmont Hotel in West Harwich, MA; wins *Mademoiselle* short fiction contest for "Sunday at the Minton's"; moves from Haven to Lawrence House at Smith; Dick Norton enters rehabilitation in upstate New York to treat exposure to tuberculosis; meets Myron "Mike" Lotz, relationship with Dick Norton is strained; visits Dick Norton at Ray Brook, NY, breaks leg in skiing accident. |
| 1953 | Simultaneously dates Myron "Mike Lotz" of Yale and Gordon Lameyer of Amherst College; writes villanelle, "Mad Girl's Love Song"; receives notification that *Harper's* accepted three poems, wins a Guest Editor position to work in June at *Mademoiselle* in New York City; lives at Barbizon Hotel in New York, writes copy for August issue of *Mademoiselle*; slowly begins falling into |

depression; in August, Plath attempts suicide by taking an overdose of sleeping pills and is missing for three days; begins treatment with Dr. Ruth Beuscher at McLean, a private mental hospital in Belmont, MA.

1954    Released and readmitted to Smith, Plath repeats the second semester of her junior year; meets Nancy Hunter, a new resident at Lawrence House; writes first poem in nearly one year; meets Richard Sassoon, a Yale student; attends Harvard Summer School, Cambridge, MA; begins senior year at Smith and thesis on Dostoevsky.

1955    Competes in Glascock Poetry Contest at Mount Holyoke College, meets Lynne Lawner; accepted to Cambridge University on Fulbright Scholarship; on June 6, Plath graduates from Smith College, *summa cum laude*; in September, she sails on the *Queen Elizabeth* to England; registers in England as a resident alien, begins courses at Newnham College, Cambridge.

1955–6  Travels in Paris and the south of France with Richard Sassoon.

1956    Attends party at Falcon Yard, meets Edward James "Ted" Hughes; on June 16, Plath marries Ted Hughes at St. George-the-Martyr in London; they honeymoon in Benidorm, Spain, and meet Warren in Paris; begins her second year at Newnham College; moves into 55 Eltisley Avenue with Hughes.

1957    Hughes's poetry collection *The Hawk in the Rain* wins Harper's poetry prize; Plath is offered position on Smith College English faculty; finishes the program at Newnham College, sails to New York City with Hughes.

1958    Leaves teaching position at Smith; receives first *New Yorker* acceptances for "Mussel Hunter at Rock Harbor" and "Nocturne"; begins seeing Dr. Beuscher, records details of visits in journals.

1959    Audits Robert Lowell's poetry course at Boston University, meets poetess Anne Sexton; visits father's grave for the first time in Winthrop with Hughes; travels across the country with Hughes; they sail for England in December.

1960    Signs contract with Heinemann in London to publish her first collection of poetry, *The Colossus and Other Poems*, on April 1, daughter Frieda Rebecca is born; *The Colossus* is published in England.

1961    Suffers from a miscarriage and appendectomy; writes "Morning Song," "In Plaster," "Tulips," "The Moon and the Yew Tree," and her novel *The Bell Jar*; Plath and Hughes settle on a house called Court Green in North Tawton, Devonshire; Plath's short story "The Perfect Place" is published in *My Weekly*.

1962    Son Nicholas Farrar is born; writes many poems including, "Three Woman," "Elm," and "The Rabbit Catcher"; tension builds in the marriage; Hughes begins having an affair with Assia Wevill; he leaves Court Green; Hughes and Plath visit Ireland, Hughes leaves abruptly; Plath rents a flat at 23 Fitzroy Road in London, formerly a residence of idol W.B. Yeats.

1963    *The Bell Jar* is published by Heinemann under the pseudonym Victoria Lucas; begins writing poetry again and writes last known poems; stays with friends Jillian and Gerry Becker; on February 11, Sylvia Plath protects the children then committs suicide by gas poisoning; she is buried in Heptonstall, England.

*The Colossus and Other Poems* (1962)

*Ariel* (1965)

*Uncollected Poems* (1965)

*Child* (1971)

*Crossing the Water* (1971)

*Crystal Gazer and Other Poems* (1971)

*Fiesta Melons* (1971)

*Lyonnesse* (1971)

*Million Dollar Month* (1971)

*Winter Trees* (1971)

*Pursuit* (1973)

*The Bed Book* (1976)

*Two Poems* (1980)

*Two Uncollected Poems* (1980)

*A Day in June* (1981)

*Dialogue over a Ouija Board* (1981)

*The Green Rock* (1982)

*The Journals of Sylvia Plath* (1982)

*Above the Oxbow* (1985)

*The Magic Mirror* (1989)

*The It-Doesn't-Matter Suit* (1996)

*The Journals of Sylvia Plath* (2000)

*Collected Children's Stories* (2001)

Aird, Eileen. *Sylvia Plath: Her Life and Work*. New York: Harper & Row, 1973. Alexander, Paul, ed. *Ariel Ascending: Writings about Sylvia Plath*. New York: Harper and Row, 1985.

Annas, Pamela J. *A Disturbance in Mirrors: The Poetry of Sylvia Plath*. New York: Greenwood Press, 1988.

Axelrod, Stephen Gould. *Sylvia Plath: The Wound and the Cure of Words*. Baltimore: The Johns Hopkins University Press, 1990.

Bassnett, Susan. *Sylvia Plath*. Totowa: Barnes and Noble Books, 1987.

Brain, Tracy. *The Other Sylvia Plath*. London: Pearson, 2001.

Bundtzen, Lynda K. *The Other Ariel*. Amherst: University of Massachusetts Press, 2001.

Butscher, Edward. *Sylvia Plath: Method and Madness*. New York: Seabury Press, 1976.

Connell, Elaine. *Sylvia Plath: Killing the Angel in the House*, 2nd ed. Hebden Bridge: Pennine Pens, 1998.

Davison, Peter. *The Fading Smile: Poets in Boston from Robert Lowell to Sylvia Plath*. New York: W. W. Norton, 1994.

Haberkamp, Frederike. *Sylvia Plath: The Poetics of Beekeeping*. Salzburg: Salzburg University Press, 1997.

Hall, Caroline King Barnard. *Sylvia Plath, Revised*. New York: Twayne, 1998.

Hargrove, Nancy D. *The Journey Toward* Ariel. Lund: Lund University Press, 1994.

Hayman, Ronald. *The Death and Life of Sylvia Plath*. New York: Birch Lane Press, 1991.

Helle, Anita. 'Family Matters: An Afterword on the Biography of Sylvia Plath'. *Northwest Review* 26 (1988, pp. 148–160).

Hughes, Ted. *Birthday Letters*. London: Faber and Faber, 1998.

———. *Crow*. London, Faber and Faber, 1970.

———. *Lupercal*. London: Faber and Faber, 1960.

———. *The Hawk in the Rain*. London: Faber and Faber, 1957.

Kendall, Tim. *Sylvia Plath: A Critical Study*. London: Faber and Faber, 2001.

Klein, Elinor. "A Friend Recalls Sylvia Plath". *Glamour 56* (Nov. 1966, pp. 168, 182–4).

Kroll, Judith. *Chapters in a Mythology*. New York: Harper and Row, 1976.

Kruh, David. *Always Something Doing*. Boston: Northeastern University Press, 1999.

Lawner, Lynne. *Triangle Dreams*. New York: Harper & Row, 1969.

———. *Wedding Night of a Nun*. Boston: Little, Brown, 1964.

Lowell, Robert. *Life Studies*. New York: Farrar, Straus, Giroux, 1959.

Macpherson, Pat. *Reflecting on* The Bell Jar. London: Routledge, 1991.

Markey, Janice. *A Journey Into the Red Eye: The Poetry of Sylvia Plath—a Critique*. London: The Women's Press, 1993.

Marsack, Robyn. *Sylvia Plath*. Buckingham: Open University Press, 1992.

Matovich, Robert. *A Concordance to the Collected Poems of Sylvia Plath*. New York: Garland Publishing, 1986.

Middlebrook, Diane. *Her Husband*. New York: Penguin, 2003.

Moses, Kate. *Wintering*. London, Sceptre Press, 2003.

Peel, Robin. *Writing Back: Sylvia Plath and Cold War Politics*. Madison: Fairleigh Dickinson University Press, 2002.

Rose, Jacqueline. *The Haunting of Sylvia Plath*. London: Virago Press, 1991.

Ruland, Wilhelm. *Legends of the Rhine*. Köln Am Rhein: Verlag von Hoursch and Bechstedt, No date.

Saldivar, Toni. *Sylvia Plath: Confessing the Fictive Self*. New York: Lang, 1992.

Strangeways, Al. *Sylvia Plath: The Shaping of Shadows*. Madison: Fairleigh Dickinson University Press, 1998.

Uroff, Margaret Dickie. *Sylvia Plath and Ted Hughes.* Urbana: University of Illinois Press, 1979.

Van Dyne, Susan R. *Revising Life: Sylvia Plath's Last Poems.* Chapel Hill: The University of North Carolina Press, 1993.

Wagner-Martin, Linda. (ed.) *Critical Essays on Sylvia Plath.* Boston: G.K. Hall and Company 1984.

————. (ed.) *Sylvia Plath: The Critical Heritage.* London and New York: Routledge, 1988.

Wagner-Martin, Linda. *Sylvia Plath: A Biography.* New York: Simon and Schuster 1987.

————. *The Bell Jar: A Novel of the Fifties.* New York: Twayne, 1992.

## WEBSITES

**"A celebration, this is":**
http://www.sylviaplath.info (the author's website)

**Academy of American Poets:**
http://www.poets.org/poets/index.cfm

**Modern American Poetry:**
http://www.english.uiuc.edu/maps/poets/m_r/plath/plath.htm

**Plath Online:**
http://www.plathonline.com/

**The English Heritage:**
http://www.english-heritage.org.uk/

**The Sylvia Plath Forum:**
http://www.sylviaplathforum.com

Plath, Otto Emil, (father of
   Sylvia), 9
   his death, 13
   expert on bees, 10
   his illness, 12
   and teacher, 10
*Plath's Incarnations,* (Bundtzen), 131
Plath, Sylvia
   accepted at Cambridge, 47
   accepted at Oxford, 48
   her attempt at suicide, 40–42
   her birth, 9
   and birth of her daughter, 84–85
   the blue plaque, 130
   on critics and her works, 4
   and 'cult' author, 3
   her depression, 116–118
   estate of, 120
   the Fulbright Scholarship, 50, 52
   her genius I.Q., 20
   and gifted poet, 1
   and going back to London, 81
   as Guest Editor for *Mademoiselle,*
      35, 37–40
   her honors, 15–17, 19, 49, 124
   as icon, 3, 5
   her life and work connected, 2, 4,
      28–29
   and marriage to Hughes, 62–63
   member of the press board,
      29–30
   the move to North Tawton,
      96–97
   her non-fiction, 127–128
   her poetry, 122–125
   her prose, 125–126
   and rejections, 110, 113
   respect for the ocean, 11
   her return to Smith College, 43
   her schooling, 12, 14
   her suicide, 1, 3, 118–119
   summer camps attended, 14, 16
   her teaching, 69–70
   on themes of her poetry, 3

   her trip to France, 56–57
   Woolf's influence on her, 5
   and writing style, 25–26
Plath, Warren Joseph, (brother of
   Sylvia), 10, 66
"Poem," 12
"Poem for a Birthday," 79, 82
*Poetry,* (magazine), 63
'Poets on Campus,' 38–39
"Point Shirley," 76
"Poppies in July," 104
Powley, Betsy, 16, 18
Prouty, Olive Higgins, 22. 32. 42
"Pursuit," 58, 61

*Queen Elizabeth,* (ship), 51, 66

"Rabbit Catcher, The," 102, 104
Ran, Shilamit, 130–131
Ratcliffe, Chris, 129
Reed, Alastair, 38
*Revising Life,* (van Dyne), 131
*Rewards of a New England Summer,*
   (article), 21
Riding, Laura, 100–101
"Rival, The," 93
Robert W. Woodruff Library,
   (Emory University), 7–8
Roche, Clarissa, 54, 71
Roethke, Theodore, 79, 89
Rorem, Ned, 7
Rosenberg, Ethel, 39
Rosenberg, Julius, 39
Ross, David, 6, 61
Rukeyser, Muriel, 7
Rumens, Carol, 7

*Saint Botolph's Review,* (magazine),
   57, 61
Salinger, J.D., 92, 125
Sarton, May, 38

PETER KEATING STEINBERG received a Bachelor of Arts in English from Mary Washington College in Fredericksburg, Virginia, in May 1996. He has been studying Sylvia Plath since 1994 and has maintained the website "A celebration, this is" since 1998. The website is located on the internet at http://www.sylviaplath.info. He has been acknowledged for his work in *Sylvia Plath: Killing the Angel in the House* by Elaine Connell and *The Unabridged Journals of Sylvia Plath* edited by Karen V. Kukil; and has been asked to review books about Sylvia Plath. He resides in Boston.

Most noted for her groundbreaking biography on Sylvia Plath, LINDA-WAGNER-MARTIN is the Frank Borden Hanes Professor of English and Comparative Literature at the University of North Carolina, Chapel Hill. She is the editor and author of over 50 books, including her recent titles *The Portable Edith Wharton* and *William Faulkner: Six Decades of Criticism*. She is also the author of biographies on Gertrude Stein and Ellen Glasgow.